AMAZING NEW ZEALAND

A.H.&A.W. REED

WELLINGTON/AUCKLAND/SYDNEY/MELBOURNE

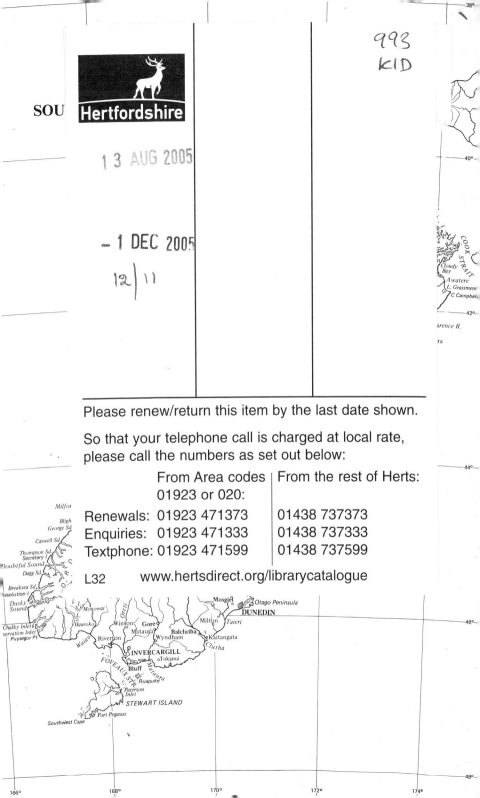

993
KID

SOU **Hertfordshire**

Please renew/return this item by the last date shown.

So that your telephone call is charged at local rate, please call the numbers as set out below:

	From Area codes 01923 or 020:	From the rest of Herts:
Renewals:	01923 471373	01438 737373
Enquiries:	01923 471333	01438 737333
Textphone:	01923 471599	01438 737599

L32   www.hertsdirect.org/librarycatalogue

AMAZING
NEW ZEALAND
A.L. Kidson

First published 1971

A. H. & A. W. REED LTD.
182 Wakefield Street, Wellington
29 Dacre Street, Auckland
165 Cashel Street, Christchurch
51 Whiting Street, Artarmon, Sydney
357 Little Collins Street, Melbourne

ISBN 0 589 00633 9

Jacket: Trinity Terrace, a colourful feature in the Waimangu
Thermal Valley, Rotorua.
Photo: *National Publicity Studios.*

The jacket and title page were designed by Trevor Plaisted;
the endpaper maps are by Julius Petro.

Set by Typemasters Ltd, Auckland
printed by
Dai Nippon Printing Co. (International) Ltd., Hong Kong

Dedication
To my wife and children

Contents

List of Illustrations

All photographs, except where otherwise stated, are by courtesy of *National Publicity Studios.*

Colour Illustrations

Acknowledgments

In deriving his facts the author has ransacked sources too numerous to acknowledge, even if he could remember all or half of them. He is specially indebted, however, to Mr E. S. Dollimore, F.R.G.S., for giving the entire script a thorough rakeover, and to the following for their vetting of different sections: Dr R. A. Falla, F.R.G.S, Dr Mervyn McLean (University of Auckland), Messrs J. H. Moreland (Dominion Museum), J. M. McEwen (Secretary, Department of Maori and Island Affairs), Don Reid (Resident Commissioner, Chatham Islands), Richard Sharell (Eastbourne), and Rex Forrester (authority on hunting and fishing, Rotorua).

Thanks are also due for permission to quote from the *Evening Post*, Wellington, the *Journal of the Polynesian Society*, the *New Zealand Herald*, the *New Zealand Weekly News*, the *Star*, Auckland, James Drummond's *Nature in New Zealand* (Whitcombe & Tombs Ltd.), Dr M. I. Soper's *More New Zealand Portraits* (Whitcombe and Tombs Ltd.), Haakon Mielche's *Round the World with the Galathea* (William Hodge & Co. Ltd.), the *New Zealand Official Year Book* (Government Printer), and Dr T. Barrow's *The Decorative Arts of the New Zealand Maori* (A. H. & A. W. Reed Ltd.).

Introduction

NEW ZEALANDERS call their homeland "God's own country". Others have dubbed it a limited utopia, a mousetrap for small men, a baby suffering from hardening of the arteries — slurs dismissed locally as "belly-aching".

But whether one swears by New Zealand or at it, the fact remains that nowhere else do so many attractions, so many natural marvels, many of them unique, jostle so close together. In its 104,000 square miles of territory — roughly the size of Britain or the State of Colorado — New Zealand presents a whole world in one country.

It has fiords, lakes, volcanoes; alpine playgrounds broader than all Switzerland; bustling modern ports and cities; first-rate farmlands, vineyards, orchards; primeval forests and vast planted ones; weird thermal regions; glow-worm grottoes, limestone caverns, and mighty reservoirs of underground steam, now used to heat homes and factories and to generate electricity.

All these, together with an extra-long coastline with sounds, fiords, gulfs and broad sandy beaches provide facilities for every kind of sport and make New Zealand a unique tourist playground.

As for climate, you can take your choice, from the subtropical to the subantarctic. Some parts have more annual sunshine than Spain or Italy. Others are snow-covered for months in the year. Rainfall varies from a scant dozen inches annually in Central Otago to more than twenty feet in other places. But most lowland areas enjoy a mild equable climate with moderate rainfall well distributed throughout the year and an abundance of sunshine.

Another unusual aspect of New Zealand is the accessibility of its many attractions. All can be reached easily and cheaply, enjoyed by young and old, rich or poor, though the very rich and the very poor are rare enough in a "welfare state" which has sometimes led the world in social legislation.

In little more than 100 years New Zealand has developed a comparatively classless community where citizens are treated according to their merit, be they Maori or pakeha (white man), Moslem or Jew. True, there are restrictions on permanent entry; but within the country there are no discriminatory laws, and very few cases of discrimination, although in any community some people will always discriminate, on the grounds of race, colour, religion, wealth, or social custom. Internal communications are highly developed and kept up-to-date. Government is stable, the populace peaceable, the general tempo of life calm and unhurried; thus the stage is well set for happy living, whether as resident or visitor.

Greatest boon of all, perhaps, is the country's uncrowded-ness, the sense of space or *lebensraum*, where less than three million people are widely dispersed over two main islands. Most of the terrain comprises farmlands, forests, mountains and sea coast, five million acres (one-thirteenth of the total land area) set aside as National Parks. Yet for all that the population is urban, not rural, in character. For although New Zealand's national income derives mainly from its farms, forests and fisheries, only a small percentage of the people are employed in primary production.

Most live in small towns of from 1,000 to 20,000 scattered all over the country, or in the score or so "cities" which have over 20,000 people. The largest is Auckland, which passed the half-million mark in the late 1960s and is still growing rapidly. Next comes the thriving South Island city of Christchurch, gateway to the Antarctic, with a 1968 population of 256,000, followed by New Zealand's capital, Wellington, with 173,000.

Six cities have their own universities and teachers' colleges and there are schools of agriculture, engineering, medicine, dentistry, pharmacy, food technology, and so on. Thus it can be seen that this country is far from being a cultural desert, which might be supposed because of its distance from great world centres. It is probably, per capita, the world's biggest buyer of books. Its education system ranks with the world's best, and its university degrees have high international standing.

New Zealanders, both Maori and pakeha, have gained world prominence in such fields as art (Frances Hodgkins), literature

(Katherine Mansfield), ballet (Rowena Jackson), historical research (Professor John Beaglehole), anthropology (Te Rangihiroa; European name, Sir Peter Buck), grand opera (Rosina Buckman, Oscar Natzke, Inia Te Wiata), plastic surgery (Sir Harold Gillies, Sir Archibald McIndoe), child rearing (Sir F. Truby King), athletics (John Lovelock, Peter Snell), rowing (D'Arcy Hadfield, Richard Arnst), boxing (Robert Fitzsimmons), warfare (Lord Freyberg), rugby football (George Nepia, Wilson Whineray, and others), education (Clarence Beeby), hydro-electric engineering (Sir William Hudson), political cartooning (David Low), nuclear fission (Lord Rutherford), and jet propulsion (Professor William Pickering), to mention only some.

With such leaders, and many others of similar calibre, working faithfully and without ostentation for the good of their country, it is not surprising to find that New Zealand enjoys a standard of living and an average family income among the best in the world. Government legislation ensures that educational, recreational and welfare facilities are available to all at a minimal cost to the individual, and a not-too-heavy tax slug.

Most families own motor cars; some have two, or even three. Highways, railways, bus and air services are all highly developed on modern lines. And so, as the spirit moves, one can mix with one's fellows, study, worship, commune with the arts, or quickly "get away from it all" — go bush, go fishing, hunting, skiing, surfing; dally on lakes and rivers, or put to sea in a boat.

For those who like to congregate there are well-appointed restaurants, dance halls, concert chambers, cinemas, and innumerable fine churches, many with historic and architectural interest. Even the smallest New Zealand village has its school and public playing fields where budding All Blacks practise from the age of eight or nine to ensure that their country retains world supremacy at rugby football; and in most districts the devotees of other sports can watch or play such games as association football, rugby league, hockey, basketball, softball, cricket, tennis, and so on.

Horse-racing ties with rugby as a national pastime, and followers of form will recall such famous New Zealanders as

Carbine, Phar Lap, Desert Gold, and Kindergarten. Many New Zealand-bred horses have won the Melbourne Cup, three of them (Hi-Jinx, Howsie and Ilumquh) passing the post with only their heads in advance of each other in the Centenary Melbourne Cup of 1960. Others have gained successes in England, India, and the United States, a recent example being the great pacer, Cardigan Bay, which became the first harness horse ever to win a million dollars in stakes.

New Zealand also has many fine golf courses, rarely if ever crowded, except perhaps at the nineteenth hole! Which reminds us that the liquor laws have lately been revised and liberalised. So today there is much less "moaning at the bar" on account of poor service, and practically none of the shoving and jostling, the swilling and spilling, for which New Zealand pubs were once well known.

All the larger centres and most tourist resorts now have up-to-date hotel accommodation, while at some — Rotorua, for example — imposing new buildings and well-trained staff provide service and amenities of international standard. Public bars close at 10 pm, but diners at licensed restaurants, and in hotels, may be served with liquor until 11.30 pm.

CHAPTER ONE

Volcanoes From Sea to Sea

NEW ZEALAND VOLCANOES form part of a vast chain girdling the Pacific, and while they do not match in size the fiery giants of Hawaii or Mexico, they are unique for their number and their variety. Auckland Isthmus, for example, has more than forty small volcanoes, some in their pristine state, others eroded or denuded, all obligingly quiet.

Over and around them sprawls the city of Auckland, New Zealand's largest metropolis; and it has been noted that in no other city or state do so many people live on, in and around volcanoes, or use them so extensively as public parks and playgrounds.

Back in 1858 — only yesterday in time, but near the beginning of New Zealand's recorded history — a visiting Austrian scientist, Dr Ferdinand Ritter von Hochstetter, recorded that the remarkable extinct volcanoes on Auckland Isthmus are unique in their number, in the peculiar shape of their cones, and the nature of their craters and lava streams.

"They are volcanoes on the smallest scale," he wrote, "cones only 300 to 600 feet in height. The highest of them, Rangitoto, which rises at the entrance of Auckland Harbour, as if it were the Vesuvius of the Waitemata, reaches a height of 900 feet. But they are real model volcanic cones and craters."

The many that remain are still tiny perfect miniatures. Yet viewed from the sea, or from ground-level, they are distinctive and impressive. They dominate the Auckland skyline as Mount Lycabettus and the Acropolis dominate that of Athens, or as the seven famous hills distinguish Rome.

Radio-carbon dating supports the theory that these Auckland volcanoes resulted from small unspectacular explosions occurring over a period of about 50,000 years. Magma (molten rock) forced up through the earth's crust from some thirty miles down, struggled to the surface where, with its energy almost spent, it erupted in a kind of weak volcanic burp. These eruptions, it is thought, lasted no more than a few minutes or a few hours, the longest being over, probably, in a matter of days.

In the fierce tribal warfare which once raged all over the Auckland Isthmus, the Maori, who had no iron or other metals, scarped and terraced many of the volcanoes for use as forts. Trenches were dug and palisades erected. Food supplies were kept in pits and storehouses on the summit, where the garrison lived and where their families usually sheltered in times of war.

Such hilltop fortresses, called *pas* (or, more correctly, *pa*) were built by different tribes throughout the country and were virtually impregnable. A number of good examples still remain. Others have been damaged, some totally destroyed, by quarrying and other modern activities, despite the protests of enlightened citizens and the efforts of an Historic Places Trust, created by Act of Parliament in 1954.

The loftiest peak in the Auckland area is Mount Eden (called by the Maoris Maungawhau) whose base and lower slopes are now covered by the homes and businesses of a populous inner suburb. A fine motor road winds up to the 644-foot summit, from which one gets a magnificent bird's-eye view of the city, its harbour (which handles about one-third of all New Zealand's sea freight) and the unrivalled Hauraki Gulf, one of the world's finest maritime playgrounds, alive with yachts for most of the year, and studded with more than forty islands.

From that summit, also, one can view the panorama of Auckland's miniature volcanoes spanning from sea to sea across the narrowest part of the country, and one can peer down, or even descend, into the depths of a volcanic crater which forms a vast natural amphitheatre.

Quite the most distinctive of the Auckland volcanoes, and the first one seen by most visitors to New Zealand, is the island mountain, Rangitoto (854 ft). Appearing almost perfectly symmetrical, Rangitoto guards the entrance to Auckland's Waitemata Harbour where it serves as a beacon for incoming ships and a barrier against north-easterly storms. Although only five miles from Auckland City, and closer still to the populous marine suburbs of Milford and Takapuna, Rangi has very few permanent residents.

Native bush covers its surface almost completely from summit to coastline, and no substantial depth of soil has yet been formed there; for Rangi is the youngest of the Auckland volcanoes, its age being assessed by carbon-dating at a mere 700 to 800 years. Thus it was no doubt seen in eruption by the Maoris, a fact suggested by the mountain's name, which means "blood-red sky". No European has ever witnessed an eruption in the Auckland area; but scientists believe that there could be further outbreaks, either through existing comes or with the formation of new ones. Future eruptions there are not thought likely to be cataclysmic.

The Bigger Blokes

Further south, on a series of geological fault zones which bisect the North Island along its northeast-southwest axis, there is a region of continuous volcanic activity. This is the Taupo Volcanic Zone, in which lie New Zealand's five active volcanoes, Rotorua, and the largest and hottest of the thermal springs. The faults continue into the Pacific as a line of active volcanoes extending from White Island to Samoa.

Inland, almost at the centre of the North Island and midway between the cities of Auckland and Wellington, stand that magnificent trio Ruapehu (9,175 ft), Ngauruhoe (7,515 ft) and Tongariro (6,458 ft), all of them active, and all within the vast area of the Tongariro National Park. Skirting the mountains is the so-called Desert Road, which crosses many miles of volcanic wasteland. From it the traveller can get a close-up view of all three mountains, towering snow-topped above the waters of Lake Taupo.

At holidays and weekends, especially in spring and winter, gay, ski-toting commuters from as far away as Auckland, Wellington, New Plymouth and Napier — virtually "all four corners" of the North Island — flock to these mountains. For, unlike mountain areas in most other countries, this alpine resort is reached quickly, easily and inexpensively, either by road or railway. Many people fly there.

Over the past 100 years Ruapehu has erupted more than twenty times, and in recent years its crater lake has bubbled, boiled and seethed, sending up steam-clouds to a height of over

3,000 feet. These have hung above the mountain like the giant mushroom clouds of nuclear explosions. In 1969 (just before the skiing season opened) came the largest of the more recent eruptions, sending a flow of lava some distance down the mountainside and scattering ash over a wide area. One high-level building was damaged but there were no human casualties. Such outbursts are heralded by preliminary tremors and rumblings, and scientists have installed an extensive warning system; so today there is little fear of any major disaster.

In the season, visitors to the Ruapehu mountain resort number thousands daily. They are attracted mainly by the snow-fields, which provide excellent skiing, and by the magnificent native forest among which there are many tracks, well signposted, and seductive walks. Facilities include a large luxury hotel (The Chateau) with golf course and a small aerodrome for light planes; alpine villages with chalets and "skotels"; a well-equipped motor camp at lower altitude; and, for those intent on going higher at a minimum of personal effort, there are modern ski-lifts and rope tows with a capacity of over 3000 an hour. Mountaineering equipment can be hired, and regular "mountain goat" trips to the summit and the crater lake are arranged by trained professional guides.

Climbers to the summit of Ruapehu — a stiff test under some conditions, impossible in others — are rewarded by the sight of a remarkable crater lake 600 feet in diameter and 8,300 feet above sea level. Though surrounded by perpetual ice and snow, the water is usually warm, sometimes boiling. Mountaineers have been known to discard their clothing and plunge in, but they run the risk of being skinned alive, since the water can be mild in some places, scalding in others, and sometimes heavily charged with acid.

Probably the world's most eccentric lake, this one occasionally disappears. It did that in May, 1945, when lava welled up from the interior of Ruapehu and displaced the water. At other times the lake has been frozen over. Its normal outlet for overflows such as that caused by the 1945 intrusion, had been through a tunnel under the ice, leading into the Whangaehu River. But from 1945 to 1947 intermittent eruptions created a deeper crater and blocked the outlet. A barrier of scoria and volcanic debris, built up by the eruptions, caused the lake water to rise to a higher level.

Then, on Christmas Eve 1953, mounting pressure carried away the barrier and released a lahar, a torrential overflow of ice, debris and muddy water, into the Whangaehu River. Surging without warning down the mountainside, this deluge swept away a railway bridge near the village of Tangiwai, just as a passenger train, crowded with holidaymakers, was approaching at midnight. The train was wrecked, and 151 people lost their lives. By a poignant coincidence, Tangiwai means "weeping water".

Close by is Ruapehu's more active neighbour, Ngauruhoe, which frequently bursts out in spectacular eruption and is seldom without a cloud of steam issuing from the summit. Ngauruhoe's slopes are steeper, more symmetrical and less suitable for skiing than those of Ruapehu, but they attract many climbers. The natural fireworks of this classically beautiful volcano were described in a letter to the *New Zealand Herald* of 30 May 1959 by J. C. Lesnie, who gives a graphic eyewitness account:

No words can adequately describe the grandeur and sheer power displayed by the mountain during the months of June to September, 1954, when I observed and photographed, in both colour and motion, the various phases of the eruption.

During one period of 24 hours in August I saw more than a million cubic yards of lava emitted — in places 80 feet in height and over a mile long. Several weeks later, while camped on this great slag heap, I was able to boil water from the stored heat and even a year later there was still evidence of heat deep below. Giant rocks as large as five-roomed houses could be seen hurtling down the mountainside and shattering into thousands of bright orange bullets, in full sunlight.

The spectacle known as lava fountaining is something which must be seen to be believed and is surely one of the grandest of all natural phenomena.

Man may explode atom bombs in a momentary exhibition of power, but volcanoes can erupt for many months with an output equivalent to thousands of such bombs.

In the past 120 years about sixty eruptions of Ngauruhoe have occurred, notably the 1954-55 series when many lava flows poured down the mountain — their total was officially estimated at about 8,000,000 cubic yards — and a large hillock of scoria almost completely filled the main crater. Lava fountaining was reported on several occasions, and there were many sharp explosions accompanied by massive discharges of ash.

The third mountain, Tongariro, now the smallest of the trio, was formerly much higher, until, countless years ago, it "blew its top" in a cataclysmic outburst which left the shattered remnant truncated and smoking. Today the broad summit, five miles long and two miles wide, contains many craters, some of which occasionally erupt. On the northern slopes, some 2,000 feet below, is Ketetahi, an area of fumaroles, boiling springs, and other thermal activity.

This mountain gives its name to the Tongariro National Park (166,561 acres), the first of many such reserves which have now been set aside for public enjoyment. A lead was given in 1887 when Te Heuheu Tukino and a group of associated chiefs presented the three great volcanoes to the nation, to be, in their words, "a national park for the benefit of everybody".

The gift was made soon after the close of a long period of hostilities between Maori and pakeha, and it is all the more remarkable since the peaks were regarded as *tapu* (sacred) by the Maori people. Within the park area are 150,000 acres of indigenous forest, lakes, glaciers, cascading streams, and warm springs mild enough to bathe in.

Next to be constituted was the Egmont National Park (82,280 acres) which also consists of a group of volcanoes and an area of land surrounding them. Most impressive, and easily overtopping the others is Mount Egmont (8,260 ft) believed by many people to be one of the world's most symmetrical mountains and often described as "New Zealand's Fujiyama". Authorities point out, however, that the symmetrical cones of both Egmont and Fujiyama are characteristic of andesite volcanoes all over the world, and that Egmont's height is about the average of similar volcanoes.

Close to the seaport city of New Plymouth, Egmont dominates the rich rolling dairylands of Taranaki Province and on clear days is visible from more than 100 miles away. The mountain thus provides a splendid natural beacon for shipping and aircraft and is often the first part of New Zealand that a traveller sees when approaching, and the last when he leaves. Less conspicuous are the two flanking features, Kaitake (2,240 ft) to the north, and Pouakai (4,590 ft) to the south. Both are volcanic in origin, and considerably older than Egmont. They have been described as "much eroded remnants". Between them is another small volcano, Pukeiti, which is now being developed as a rhododendron garden by the New Zealand Rhododendron Trust.

Captain James Cook sighted Egmont on 10 January 1770 and named it in honour of the Earl of Egmont, then First Lord of the Admiralty. The Maoris called this mountain Taranaki, and according to their lore its peak was *tapu*, and the home of a legendary ancestor. Ancient burial caves have been found on the mountainside, containing human skeletons and native implements.

Maori tradition attributes the first ascent to an oldtime chief, Tahurangi, who climbed from a native village which once stood on the site of the present North Egmont Chalet. When he reached the top, it is said, this chief lit a fire to show that he had accomplished the climb and taken possession of the peak. And so it became a custom with the local Maoris, when they saw thin wisps of vapour encircle Egmont's summit and blow away from it like smoke upon the breeze, to exclaim: "*Ae, te ahi a Tahurangi!*" ("Look, there is Tahurangi's fire!")

The first European ascent was made in December 1839 by Dr Ernst Dieffenbach, a German naturalist employed by the New Zealand Company. He was accompanied by a whaler named Heberley. But due to the *tapu* the party encountered difficulties with their Maori guides and porters, who could not be induced to proceed beyond a certain point. The names Tahurangi Bluff and Dieffenbach Cliffs on Egmont commemorate the first Maori and the first pakeha to conquer the cone.

Several translations are quoted for the Maori name Taranaki. One of them, given on good authority, is "the barren or treeless mountain"; but this is very much a misnomer, since heavy forest clothes the lower slopes of Egmont, and formerly this forest swept down almost to the sealine. Vast tracts still extend up to and beyond the 3,000-foot level. Above that the vegetation becomes progressively smaller, with low scrub, tussock, moss and lichens interspersed with ranunculus, celmisia and other alpine flowers. Then comes bare rock, scoria screes, fields of dazzling snow and ice. In winter all is covered with a thick mantle of snow, from base to summit.

On fine days the eighteen-mile drive from New Plymouth to the North Egmont Chalet at 3,140 feet is a memorable experience, with the mountain in full view all the way, except for the last few miles when the road winds up through the forest, and tantalising vistas of peak and snowfield, or of rugged torrent-torn gorges, may be glimpsed through the trees. Other approaches, similarly fascinating, are to the Dawson Falls Hostel at 2,970 feet, from Hawera (twenty-seven miles) or Stratford (fifteen miles); and to the Stratford Mountain House at 2,775 feet. All three have permanent hotel accommodation for tourists and climbers, and there are numerous trampers' huts. Egmont also has its popular ski grounds (though less developed and less extensive than those on Ruapehu) with ski tows at several places.

In summer the ascent of Egmont is an easy scramble, taking only a few hours; and it has been claimed that more people stand on the summit of Egmont each year than on any other comparable peak. Infants in arms have been carried there; and from time to time the inevitable "stuntists", record-breakers, and ill-prepared adventurers cause concern to genuine mountaineers, who are called on to risk their own lives in the process of rescue and extrication.

For, with all her attractions, Egmont also has her perils, which should not be taken lightly. The weather there can change very quickly, from bright sunshine to dense fog, or from mild warmth to freezing cold. Winter climbing is mostly a matter of ice-axe and crampons; and, with inclines of up to 50 degrees and many perpendicular faces, Egmont in winter presents a stiff challenge to experts.

It is not surprising, then, that tragedies occur on the easy-seeming slopes of Egmont, such as that of July 1953 when a large party slipped on an upper ice slope and six people lost their lives. Among the earliest fatalities was that of a Wellington man, who in April 1891 made a lone ascent — a dangerous practice now forbidden on Egmont. It is surmised that when near the summit he slipped and fell. Ten months later his body was discovered in a perfect state of preservation, even the moustaches and eye-lashes being intact. Successive layers of ice and snow which had covered the body were only then beginning to thaw.

Today this mountain, with its numerous tracks and bush walks, is well signposted and has many warning notices for the uninitiated. Various alpine clubs in the surrounding province have evolved a system of organised search and rescue, with portable radios and other modern equipment. This and some high-level shelters, notably the well-provided Syme Hut at 6,439 feet, reduces the risk and adds to the popularity of Egmont as a mountain resort.

Throughout the period of European settlement Egmont has remained quiescent, and is commonly thought to be extinct. Experts, however, now class this volcano as "dormant" i.e. sleeping. There is definite evidence of a series of outbursts 350 years ago, while some scientists believe that the mountain was still erupting less than 200 years ago and is likely to do so again, probably with considerable violence. A leading New Zealand geologist, however, has declared that an eruption of Egmont would probably do more good than harm through the fertilising effect of the resultant ash showers. People, he says, should pray daily for this mountain to erupt again!

A prominent feature on Egmont's southern flank is Fantham Peak, a perfect example of the parasitic cone — a mountain which has grown upon the side of another and used the volcanic substance of its host for nourishment. In bygone ages, Egmont's pipe or vent became blocked with solidified lava. Subsequent activity lacked sufficient force to eject the blockage or to lift the top off the mountain, so it found a weak spot in the side and blew out there. At 6,438 feet above sea level and about a mile below the summit of Egmont, Fantham Park can be reached by a 3,000-foot climb from the Dawson Falls Hostel. It is now a popular venue for skiing and other winter sports, and a large mountain hut has been built there.

The most destructive New Zealand eruption of modern times occurred on 10 June 1886 when Mount Tarawera (3,770 ft), twenty miles from the town of Rotorua, suddenly exploded after lying dormant for about 900 years. Tarawera's three age-old craters, probably plugged by solidified lava, were unable to cope with this new access of colossal energy, so the mountain blew itself apart. A line of new craters opened up a great rift running southwest to northeast along its whole length, from which were ejected blocks, scoria, ash and mud, spewed over some 6,000 square miles of farmland and forest.

This outburst came on a cold moonlit night in mid-winter, accompanied by earthquakes and loud detonations which were heard as far away as Auckland. The affected area contained three Maori villages, all of which were destroyed with heavy loss of life. The precise death roll will never be known, but it is generally accepted that 147 Maoris and six Europeans perished in that night of terror. Survivors had to battle their way across miles of once-familiar territory now changed beyond recognition, with all the old landmarks obliterated and vast new featutes confronting them at every turn.

Activity extended to nearby Lake Rotomahana, whose 284 acres of shallow water completely disappeared. The lake bed, formerly at a depth of about thirty feet, subsided to 250 feet, and opened up with craters, geysers, and bubbling mud pools which continued for about seven years when the waters returned to form a new lake twenty times the extent of the original one. In addition to the human tragedy and the destruction of property, the Tarawera eruption of 1886 caused an irreparable scenic disaster by obliterating the famous Pink and White Terraces, silicate formations whose form and beauty had no counterpart anywhere in the world.

The smallest and most turbulent of New Zealand's active volcanoes is White Island, a miniature Stromboli about 1000 feet high, thirty miles off the coast of Poverty Bay, and at the northern end of the Taupo-Rotorua Volcanic Zone. This island has a circumference of only four miles, but it is actually the summit of a large volcano fifteen miles in diameter which has been built up from the seabed and is mostly submerged. White Island exhibits all the usual thermal phenomena of boiling pools, steam and gas vents, lakelets of acid, and so on. Large deposits of sulphur on the island were worked commercially up to September 1914, when an eruption from the crater caused a landslide and mudflow which destroyed the buildings and led to the death of twelve employees.

Scientists visiting White Island recently have recorded that there is no other volcano like it in the world. They could transport apparatus to it easily by sea, camp on the edge of the crater, and go by an easy walk every day to the steam vents. They found that the steam is corrosive to most metals, including stainless steel, and they were obliged to collect their samples in a gold-lined vessel costing 100 dollars. They noted a group of sulphur mounds containing molten sulphur which could be bailed out with a dipper, a fearsome fumarole named Noisy Nellie which created a terrific din, and a small jet that spluttered raw hydrochloric acid.

Captain Cook gave the name to this island (called Whakaari by the Maoris) on 31 October 1869. He noted in his Journal: "I have named it White Island because as such it always appeared to us." Today its appearance is usually yellow, though white steam clouds often hang over it.

CHAPTER TWO

The People

IT HAS BEEN SAID that New Zealand is the only country in the world where a white race lives side by side with a coloured one on equal and harmonious terms. Two races, one people — this is the social and ethnological conundrum which has confronted New Zealand politicians and thinkers ever since William Hobson, the country's first British Consul and Lieutenant-Governor, declared the two races — Maori and European — to be one when he signed the Treaty of Waitangi in 1840.

At first the marriage was distinctly uneasy, entailing many quarrels. But the inherent good sense and the finer qualities of both parties have made for a partnership which, while still not perfect, has come to be recognised as eminently successful.

In its brief term of nationhood New Zealand has functioned as a unique social laboratory, and this young country has worked out some advanced experiments in human living and welfare. New Zealand was the first country to introduce universal franchise, and it pioneered advances in social security, in systems of arbitration to solve industrial disputes, in free and universal education, and in specialised methods for rearing and protecting infants. All this has been done while grappling with the manifold problems of settling and developing a new land.

In these and other ways New Zealand has developed its own kind of people, a quite distinctive people, broadly homogeneous and, according to many New Zealanders, "superior"! This process has been helped by the country's geographical situation — isolated in the South Pacific, more than 1000 miles from Australia, and much further from any other continent. New Zealand has never suffered the incursions of hungry hordes, hostile fleets, invading armies, or attacking aircraft. Even the atom bomb is still comfortably remote.

So this country has been able to pursue, unhindered, its own social and nationalistic ideals. It has worked out a comfortable pattern of life, with high average earnings and a narrower gap between large and small incomes than in any other Western nation.

Only two main ethnic streams have ever flowed into New Zealand — the Polynesians or Maoris from the Pacific Islands, and northern Europeans, mostly from Great Britain. Compare this with, for example, Canada, where newspapers are issued in more than forty tongues; with Australia, where migrants from many countries continue to pour in; or with the United States, where ethnic origins are even more diverse. Over the past half-century New Zealand has so controlled her flow of immigrants that today Asians, Africans, and West Indians are severely restricted in their right of permanent entry, as are the nationals of some European countries.

Racial Minorities

At one time there were many Chinese on the New Zealand goldfields; and later, in both Auckland and Wellington, "Chinatowns" lent their splashes of Oriental colour, though not to be compared of course with those of San Francisco or Vancouver. Today these have disappeared, and New Zealand's Chinese, numbering about 8,000, follow the Western mode of life.

In 1885 a Chinese storekeeper named Chew Chong bought butter from Taranaki dairy farmers and shipped two kegs of it to England. He lost money on this venture, but a few years later he opened dairy factories in Taranaki, fitting them with Danish cream separators and other up-to-date equipment. Although these were not the first dairy factories in the country (one had been established at Edendale, in Otago, as early as 1882, Chew Chong certainly helped New Zealand along the way to her present position as the world's greatest exporter of dairy produce.

Another way Chew Chong helped was by purchasing from the hard-pressed dairymen what was known as "Taranaki Wool" — an edible fungus, similar to the product eaten in China, which grew profusely on logs and stumps where farmers of the infant colony had cleared bushland to establish pastures. In those lean years the dairymen had very few sources of income. They turned in their butter, made at home by primitive methods, to the local store and took goods in exchange. To get ready money they were obliged to work on road-building or bush-felling contracts. And so the cash Chew Chong paid them for fungus, which cost nothing to produce, was a godsend, and enabled many a struggling dairy-farmer to carry on.

Today, edible fungus no longer features in the list of New Zealand exports (except perhaps as tinned mushrooms) but there is a continuing trade in "antlers in velvet", i.e. at the green and undeveloped stage, and certain other parts of the deer, which are valued in the east as aphrodisiacs. The strangest export items to pass between the two countries were cargoes of coffins containing dead Chinese which left New Zealand in the early days for reburial in the land of the deceaseds' ancestors. In 1902 the twin-screw steamer *Ventnor*, bound for Hong Kong with 499 of these caskets and a load of Westport coal, sank about ten miles from Omapere on the Hokianga Harbour. The captain and twelve of the ship's crew lost their lives when their boat was sucked under by the sinking vessel. No trace of the coffins was ever found.

In early times, along with the main flow of British migrants to New Zealand, came significant numbers from Scandinavia and other parts of Europe. Yugoslavs, Germans, French, Poles, Swiss, Dutch, and Italians have all played their part in the development of this young country; and today small ethnic communities still exist in areas where these immigrants estab-lished settlements. Although New Zealand now has strict immigration laws, the people of several Pacific Island territories which were at one stage, or still are, under New Zealand juris-diction, enjoy free right of entry. These include nationals of the Cook, Niue, and Tokelau Islands.

A Model Settlement

Right from the start New Zealand was planned as a model colony to be developed on rational lines and not just left to

Ski jumper on Mount Ruapehu, with Ngauruhoe in the distance.

A Maori carver at work in the North Island tourist town of Rotorua. Hanging on his hut are Maori kits (*kete*) and a warclub (*patu*). He is using traditional Maori tools.

Reconstruction of a Maori fortified village, or *pa* (from a painting by Marcus King). Note the precipitous sides, palisades, earthworks, and watchtower.

grow, or to perish (as so many infant colonies did) in haphazard fashion. Nor was it to be a dumping ground for convicts or other undesirables, who, in the early 1800s were all too numerous in many impoverished British cities.

The chief architect of the plan was Edward Gibbon Wakefield, a brilliant Englishman. He advanced his theories as a remedy for the social ills of that time. "Send people out of England," he urged in numerous publications and speeches, "not as convicts but as free settlers who will own their own land and work on it to support their wives and families"'

But, he insisted, colonial land should not be given indiscriminately as free grants. It should be sold to settlers at a price which would prevent labourers from becoming landowners too soon. For Wakefield believed that the proper development of a new country entailed a kind of "balanced society" wherein farmers, labourers, artisans and professional people would work together towards mutual prosperity and the common good.

From an early interest in South Australia as an area for settlement, Wakefield turned his attention in 1837 to New Zealand. He formed an Association which afterwards became the New Zealand Company, a joint stock venture, (i.e. a commercial enterprise) for the colonisation of this country. He himself went to Canada in 1838 on the invitation of the High Commissioner for British North America (Lord Durham) where he was able to influence colonial development not only through his close association with Lord Durham, but also as an elected member of the Canadian legislature, representing the French-settled county of Beauharnois.

Meanwhile his brother, Colonel William Wakefield, reached New Zealand in 1839 as Principal Agent for the New Zealand Company. He immediately began negotiations with leading Maori chiefs for the purchase of land for the first organised British settlement there. Thus it was William Wakefield who actually established the first settlements, at Wellington, Wanganui and New Plymouth; and in 1841 another brother, Captain Arthur Wakefield, established a similar settlement at Nelson. "But behind these men stood Edward Gibbon Wakefield, the arch planner and organiser, who did not himself come out to New Zealand until near the end of his life, when he took a very active if stormy part in its politics," wrote his great-grand-daughter, Miss Irma O'Connor, in a letter to the *New Zealand Herald* in 1968.

CHAPTER THREE

The Maori

TODAY NEW ZEALANDERS are a unified people, sharing comon. purposes along with equal access to schools and universities, equal status within the community, equal social and economic opportunities, and equal rights to religious and other freedoms. But this situation, largely harmonious, was not achieved easily.

In the early days there were bitter quarrels between Maori and pakeha, leading to sporadic wars — though never a full-scale one with all Maoris pitted against all pakehas. Many tribes were not affected at all; others fought on the side of the pakeha. Much Maori land was sequestered in the early days, despite the pious phrases of the Waitangi "Treaty", and Maori interests were often disregarded both through the white man's greed and through a mutual lack of understanding. This was caused largely by difficulties of communication, especially language difficulties, which concealed basic differences in social custom and in ways of thinking.

European diseases took their toll — especially the simple ones such as mumps, measles, influenza and the common cold. Scarlet fever, now mastered by medical science, tuberculosis, and the various poxes — dreadful enough for Europeans at that time — all proved highly lethal among a simple folk whose knowledge of medicine and hygiene was primitive, and whose facilities for treatment were virtually non-existent. Nor had they developed the pakeha's resistance to some of these diseases.

Then there was the white man's musket, prized above all by a warrior race whose tribes were constantly, and traditionally, feuding. Even if a few trade samples did happen to explode, through faulty mechanism or inept handling, killing the man behind the weapon instead of the one in front, shrewd chieftains such as Te Rauparaha (the "Maori Napoleon" who moved his headquarters to Kapiti Island to be near pakeha vessels which came to trade, or to capture whales) quickly appraised the musket as an unrivalled instrument for carnage and conquest.

The demon rum, copiously supplied as "payment" to an unsophisticated folk who previously knew no form of intoxicant, caused some top-rate orgies, with sore heads and broken ones resulting. How many sore and broken hearts it caused is a matter for conjecture, but there can be no doubt that the white man's liquor helped to debauch the oldtime Maori.

At the end of the nineteenth century, after only a few decades of European contact, the Maori faced extinction. Their numbers had dwindled from an estimated 250,000 to less than 45,000. The Maori was a "dying race". And those who despise the early Australian settlers for hunting and shooting Aborigines, just as they hunted and shot kangaroos or dingoes, may reflect that the Maori too was hunted by well-trained, well-fed and well-equipped regiments of British regular soldiers, supported by the Colonial Militia, by ships of the Royal Navy using rockets and artillery, by the so-called "friendly" people of their own race (meaning, of course, friendly to the British) and by parties of the Royal Marines.

The wonder is that this outstanding race survived at all. Yet today New Zealanders of predominantly Maori blood total over 220,000. Their rate of natural increase has exceeded 3 per cent in recent years, one of the highest in the world, and about twice that of the predominantly white New Zealand population.

Today many Maoris are successful farmers, and Maoris practise freely in all the trades, arts and professions, though not, pro rata, to the same extent as Europeans. It is, in fact, a matter of national concern, and especially one for the Maori leaders, that so many of their people gravitate to the unskilled occupations, while too few qualify educationally and otherwise for the "higher echelons" of employment with all their apparent economic and social advantages.

This may be because the growing Maori element in New Zealand seems determined to hold fast to its Maoriness, its maoritanga; and so the modern Maori faces a dilemma when he tries to do this and is impelled at the same time to compete with the pakeha in Western cultures and ways of living. Today several New Zealand universities include Maori studies in their curricula, and there is a plethora of Maori clubs, leagues, and organisations — all distinctive, many highly colourful and attractive.

Maoris have served with distinction in the New Zealand armed forces of both World Wars, in Japan, Korea, Vietnam and Malaysia. Four seats in the New Zealand Parliament are reserved for Maoris, to represent Maori constituencies instituted in 1867 and now considered by some to be anomalous. Maoris and part-Maoris sometimes contest the European seats.

A Maori, the late Sir James Carroll, was several times Acting Prime Minister of New Zealand. A number of others have been knighted, notably Sir Apirana Ngata, a brilliant scholar by world standards and the first of his race to gain a university degree. Both he and Sir Peter Buck (Te Rangihiroa) had distinguished political careers in New Zealand.

Sir Peter afterwards became Professor of Anthropology at Yale University and Director of Hawaii's Bernice P. Bishop Museum at Honolulu. Qualified also in medicine and surgery, this son of an Irish father and a Maori mother served both as an infantry and a medical officer in the First World War, gained the DSO, and was twice mentioned in despatches. During his lifetime (c. 1877-1951) Sir Peter received many awards and honorary degrees from overseas universities.

This distinguished Maori deduced from anthropological research that his Polynesian ancestors probably came from Asia in remote ages past, then worked their way eastward via the Indonesian islands to the central Pacific. The Polynesian language, spoken by the Maoris of New Zealand and the Cook Islands, as well as by the natives of Samoa, Tonga, Hawaii, and Easter Island, has affinities with some Indonesian dialects.

"During their stay in Indonesia," Sir Peter wrote, "the sea salt entered into their blood and changed them from landsmen to seamen. When the pressure of Mongoloid peoples pouring in from the mainland became oppressive, the Polynesians turned their gaze towards the East and started on one of the greatest adventures of man."

And so these "Vikings of the Sunrise" came to occupy that vast Pacific triangle which has at its apex the Hawaiian Islands, and at its base New Zealand and Easter Island. Of all the scattered territories within this triangle New Zealand is the largest, the latest to be settled by the Polynesians, and the furthest from their place of origin.

To reach New Zealand the Polynesians, who had no metals and could not read or write, made incredible ocean voyages of well over 1000 miles. They travelled in wooden canoes propelled by sails and paddles, with the sun, moon and stars (plus an uncanny knowledge of winds and ocean currents) as their sole navigational aids.

According to the traditional songs and stories transmitted by word of mouth from generation to generation, the first Maori to reach New Zealand was Kupe. About the year 950 AD this man was fishing near his island home, Hawaiki, in the mid-Pacific, when a great storm arose and blew him far down to the south.

Hawaiki, the immediate ancestral home of the Maori, according to their folklore, *might* have been Hawaii; but more likely it was Savai'i in Western Samoa, or Raiatea in the Society Islands. However, Kupe, alone in his canoe (so one version of the legend has it) found himself unable to battle against the storms so he went along with them. Finally he sighted a long low coastline like a cloud on the distant horizon . . . "Aotea-roa" Land of the Long White Cloud (or, as some translate it, Land of the Shining Sunrise).

The legend says that Kupe found nobody in these southern islands and, tiring of a solitary life there, he sailed away back to Hawaiki where he made known his discovery. Modern re-searchers believe that such a feat was impossible. They also point out that the earliest C.14 carbon dating for the settlement of man in New Zealand is more than 1,000 years ago, and they expect that further archaeological research will indicate even earlier settlements; so it is most likely that New Zealand was indeed inhabited by about 950 A.D., the supposed time of Kupe's arrival there.

The earliest inhabitants of whom traces have been found are classified today as Polynesians of the Archaic or Moa Hunter period. A later influx of adventurous Polynesians from the central Pacific, in or around 1350 A.D., launched the so-called classic period of Maori culture. But it is now believed that the

Polynesian settlement of New Zealand has been both sporadic and continuous. There is, in short, no foundation for the popular belief that the country was peopled by an organised expedition which came in seven or eight large canoes about 400 years after the voyage of Kupe. While the arrival of the legendary canoes (named *Te Arawa, Tokomaru, Tainui, Aotea, Kurahaupo, Takitimu, Mataatua,* and *Horouta*) is not doubted, new concepts have developed concerning the timing and purpose of their voyages.

There is little doubt, however, that the Maoris, when they did come, brought to New Zealand kumaras and other useful plants, and two kinds of four-legged animal — the dog and the rat. Before the arrival of these, the only land-dwelling mammals in New Zealand were two species of bat, colonies of which still survive. Man was a very late arrival, his advent there being the latest in any considerable land tract on this planet, with the exception of Antarctica.

The Maori rat (*kiore*) which is believed to survive still in some remote areas, probably travelled as a stowaway, hidden among the provender stored in the migrants' canoes. The dogs, no doubt, were shipped as reserve rations or as pets, or for the value of their skins, which made good cloaks. In the early Polynesian economy dogs would play little part, if any, as hunters, herders, or protectors of human beings. Today the Maori word *kuri*, meaning dog, is still quite common in New Zealand speech for any kind of canine, although no true *kuri* (Polynesian dog) can now be found.

Pigs, horses, sheep, and cows, so prominent today in the New Zealand scene and so important to the New Zealand economy, were introduced much later, as were numerous other animals, some of which have multiplied enormously, becoming destructive and costly pests.

At first the Maoris fiercely resisted the encroachment of white settlers, for their high intelligence told them that despite "treaties", "land deals" and other unfamiliar blandishments, they were doomed as a separate and independent people once their territory was alienated.

So bravely and stubbornly did they fight, and so expert were they in the arts of bushcraft and guerilla warfare, that the

British took decades to subdue them. And it is to the lasting shame of the conquerors that a wholesale confiscation of Maori lands followed the final victory. Another sour feature was the confining of Maori prisoners of war in hulks on Auckland harbour, or on small islands in the Hauraki Gulf, where a number took sick or pined away.

Before the advent of the white man's musket and *tupara* (double-barrelled gun) the Maori fought his battles hand-to-hand, using a few simple but effective weapons. These were of two types: the long club or *taiaha*, and a variety of short clubs made of wood, stone or bone and now given the generic name of *patu poto*.

Contrary to general belief the *taiaha* was not a spear. It was about five feet long and made of wood, was light to handle, and had a narrow sword-like blade. This was the "business end", which could kill or maim a man with one blow. Skill with the *taiaha* entailed constant exercise and deft movement of the feet and body. Numerous forms of thrust and parry were learned and practised, youths using the harmless but serviceable *korari* (flax-flower stalks) in their early training.

The end opposite the blade was certainly pointed, and used for jabbing. But it had no barbs and was not sharp enough for piercing. This end was carved to represent a human head with a long out-thrust tongue — the traditional token of defiance. Above the head was a band of red feathers from the *kaka* (a native bird) and a tuft of hair from the *kuri* (native dog), one purpose of this embellishment being to distract the enemy's eye.

In *The Decorative Arts of the New Zealand Maori* Dr T. Barrow writes: "The common characteristic of short clubs is a broad flat blade with a rounded end made sharp enough to split the skull of a man, or to cause deadly injuries to the neck or ribs by thrusting blows.

"All the short clubs, or *patu* as they are usually called, were designed for quick in-fighting where split-second action required thrusting jabs with little time for downward blows. The fighter kept firm hold on the weapon by means of a thong of dogskin which passed through the hole on the handle of the weapon and round his wrist and thumb.

"It was possible for a skilled warrior with a short club, by speed of action and by using a cloak wrapped around the left arm to parry blows, to defeat an opponent armed with a long club." Barrow also observes that frequently *taiaha* opened an engagement and *patu* concluded it!

Maori warriors were led by able and resolute chiefs. "We will fight you for ever and ever," defiantly answered one of them (Rewi Maniapoto) when, in a hopeless military situation, he was called upon to surrender. That was at Orakau, about a hundred miles south of Auckland, the scene of a famous battle between Maori and pakeha.

When, before that battle, a safe-conduct was offered to the women and children, a chief's wife spoke up: "If the men are to die, the women and children will die also." Yet for all his fine qualities, the old-time Maori was not the "noble savage" depicted by some observers. He had, on the contrary, some traits and customs which today are abhorred. Among them was cannibalism. "I'm Scottish by assimilation," claimed one prominent New Zealander recently; his ancestors had eaten a Presbyterian missionary. The Maori believed that if he ate the heart of a formidable foe, that man's courage would be added to his own. And so, upon the field of battle, he would hack out an enemy's heart and devour it. Or, if he wished to insult a dead foe — and so, perhaps, avenge a former insult — the warrior would gouge out his victim's eyes and swallow them.

For his more regular diet he ate fish and shellfish, *taro* and *kumara* (a species of sweet potato), fern roots, and the succulent stalks and leaves of forest plants. In a variety of ingenious ways he also caught birds, especially the plump wood pigeon, which grows bigger and fatter in New Zealand than elsewhere. These he would preserve in their own fat for future use, and he also preserved fish, his only other flesh-food apart from "long pig", by smoking and sun-drying. To catch fish the Maori used shell or bone hooks, cunningly shaped and barbed. He made lines and fishnets from the fibre of the native "flax" plant — *phormium tenax*, a species of hemp — which grows profusely in New Zealand, especially in some swamp areas. And in making his nets he used a kind of knot identical with one that was used by the prehistoric Swiss lake-dwellers.

Although the oldtime Maori used no metals, he applied high

intelligence and artistic skill to his undertakings. His tools and weapons were fashioned from bone, wood, stone or shell; and it is believed that modern man, using similar implements, would be unable to equal the Maori's performance. Almost everything he made was tastefully, often elaborately, decorated. And so he developed to a high degree several different art forms.

Pre-eminent among these was woodcarving, countless examples of which still survive, in museums, in Maori pas, and in private collections. The supports and other timbers of many Maori homes were elaborately and artistically carved, as were those of the large meetinghouse which served as a kind of "town hall" for every considerable community. There, and on the *marae*, or open space outside, matters of common import were discussed freely and democratically, as in the forums of ancient Rome.

Maori carvings often represent grotesque human figures, which are sometimes vaguely reminiscent of North American totem poles. They feature squat and heavily tattooed figures, usually with hands clasping rotund bellies. Free curvilinear patterns abound in Maori artwork, with the spiral and often the double spiral predominating, a motif gained from the fronds of the Tree Fern or the shapes of seashells.

Beautiful and intricate designs were worked out mentally for the Maori had no "blueprints" or other paper records to assist him in his artistic creations. He also decorated his own body by tattoing, the most intriguing of which was the elaborate *moko*, or facial tattoo, chiselled into the countenance of every high-born male. This also served as a chief's "identity badge"; and many who subscribed to the Treaty of Waitangi drew on that document a part of their *moko* by way of signature. To enhance their beauty, Maori women often had their chins and upper lips tattooed and sometimes also their foreheads.

The Maori carved in his distinctive style the high prows and stern-pieces of his mighty canoes, which were often fashioned from a single tree trunk and could hold as many as 100 people. Paddles and bailers, food and water containers, chests and caskets, almost everything he used, in fact, were similarly decorated.

For clothing the Maori wore cloaks and kilted skirts made from the fibre of that same "flax" plant, which he used for nets and fishlines. Maori women were skilled in preparing and weaving this fibre, and here again a high artistic standard was attained, not only in the fine quality of the weaves, but also through the use of vegetable dyes to produce attractive coloured patterns based on the triangle, the diamond and the rectangle. Delightful effects — and personal warmth — were obtained by interweaving the feathers of birds such as the kaka and the kiwi, the crimson feathers of the kaka being especially prized for this purpose. Dogs' skins provided yet another level of style and quality in the fashioning of raiment.

Personal ornaments, of which the Maori was very fond, were fashioned in a variety of forms: ear pendants and necklaces were made from shell, bone, sharks' teeth, or greenstone, and head adornments were created from plaited "flax", evergreen leaves, or bird feathers. Specially prized, and worn as a head-dress by men of high rank, were plumes from the *huia*, a bird which is now considered to be extinct.

Both sexes wore the traditional *tiki* (or *heitiki*), a carved figurine, suspended from a cord around the neck. The *tiki* is unique among Polynesian ornaments, and was thought to have supernatural powers which could bring fertility to a married woman or abundance to a planted crop if the proper rites were observed and the proper incantations chanted.

Maori Music

With their mellow voices, relaxed personalities and mature sense of rhythm, modern Maoris are "naturals" as singers and many have become adept with present-day musical instruments, especially those of the guitar and ukulele type. Maori ensembles from time to time stage concerts in cities and tourist resorts such as Rotorua. Small groups sometimes welcome and farewell overseas liners, larger ones make impressive contributions at functions in honour of distinguished visitors.

Maori clubs are numerous in the universities, teachers' colleges, secondary schools and church organisations. These groups, concerned as they are with keeping alive the old-time Maori culture, often practise and perform traditional dances and action songs such as the *poi* and the *haka*.

Maoris have also made their mark as soloists, some well-known examples being Maggie Papakura, Dean Waretini, and Ana Hato. More recently, Inia Te Wiata has played the leading role in the Broadway musical hit *Most Happy Fella* and in a New Zealand production of *Porgie and Bess;* while the lovely soprano, Kiri Te Kanawa, has starred in opera on the London stage.

Basic Maori music, however — the ancestral chants and songs in which were embodied so much of the ancient tribal lore, and which were the indispensable accompaniment to every important situation and circumstance in the life of the old-time Maori, are seldom heard now. And, when they are heard, they fail to please either the pakeha ear or that of most Maoris.

Because of their limited tone range (usually only three or four notes on our Western scale) and the absence of familiar rhythmic patterns, these ancient melodies are usually described as monotonous or doleful. Yet they are of immeasurable antiquity — perhaps the most ancient known to man. They derive from a past era when the Polynesians lived somewhere on the mainland of South-east Asia; and they survived because of the isolation afforded, for 1000 years at least, by the vast Pacific.

European discovery and settlement, of course, destroyed that isolation and submerged a great deal of the oldtime culture. But determined efforts are now being made to restore and preserve it, by collecting, tape-recording, and notating the ancient *karakia* (incantations), *waiata* (songs of love and grief), *oriori* (lullabies), and other vocal art forms.

Their number ran to thousands. One recent worker in this field (Dr Mervyn McLean, of Auckland University) had, by 1964, taped about 800 and had commenced the prodigious task of translating them into a fixed notation — a unique enterprise, and one of inestimable cultural value. Through it, genuine Maori music may again come to be heard and appreciated throughout New Zealand, perhaps even further afield.

Musical Instruments

Maori musical instruments were of two types: the flute, used to accompany chants and *waiata;* and the trumpet, whose main use was in warfare. Of the different flutes the commonest was the *koauau* — a typical narrow tube made of wood or bone, four to eight inches long, open at both ends and having from three to six fingerholes, but usually only three. Often elaborately carved, the *koauau* and other flutes were greatly prized by their owners; and it is said that Maori flute players were envied and feared because of their power over the affections of women.

One common kind of Maori trumpet was the *pumoana* (or *putara*) made from a large conch shell by cutting off the tip and fitting a wooden mouthpiece, as done in many countries from ancient times. The *pumoana* was used for signalling, and for some ceremonial purposes such as summoning people together for a meeting, to announce the birth of a high-ranking male child, or the approach of a visiting chief.

Another kind was the *pukaea* or war trumpet, a wooden instrument three to eight feet long and flared at one end to a bell of up to eight inches in diameter. According to one early writer the *pukaea* made "a very uncouth kind of braying". Another said it made "a groaning, moaning sound like the voice of a dying wild bull". It has even been likened to the sound of bagpipes!

Unlike European trumpets, and those of Tibet which it closely resembles, the *pukaea* was fitted at the bell end with carved wooden pegs called *tohe*, which are thought to represent the human tonsils. The Maori also used this instrument as a speaking trumpet — often to hurl curses at an enemy. One insult, "*To roro! To roro!*" ("Your brains! Your brains!") signified the amiable intention of the announcer to knock out the brains of his listeners.

It will be clear from all this that the Maori has contributed — and continues to contribute — a great deal to the New Zealand cultural pattern. He has a fine aesthetic sense; he shows deep spiritual qualities in his poetry, his mythology, and his traditional religious concepts; he has a strong social sense, flavoured by humour and an extrovert ebullience. Physically he is strong, virile and handsome; his intelligence matches that of the pakeha. In what he considers to be a good cause he can be loyal, aggressive, tenacious and self-sacrificing.

Thus he has made, and is still making, a unique contribution to the development of a unique nation. Not a bad record for a "dying race"!

CHAPTER FOUR

The Moriori

MUCH IS KNOWN ABOUT the New Zealand Maori, and especially about his superb arts and crafts, which have now been amply studied and documented.

But what of those mysterious, shadowy folk, the Moriori, who settled in the Chatham Islands (500 miles east of Christchurch) there to develop a culture of their own, and an art form so distinctive that it might well be classed as unique?

For a long time it was believed by Europeans, and taught in their schools, that the Moriori were a Melanesian people, with black skins and fuzzy hair, who preceded the Maori to New Zealand and were thus its first inhabitants.

According to this pretty tale, the Maori, when he arrived on the scene, promptly killed and ate most of these "first inhabitants", married a few, and so harassed the miserable remainder that some fled inland to the wild and mountainous Urewera country, while others sought refuge in the equally isolated Chathams.

Research has now established that the Maori and the so-called Moriori (the last of whom died at the Chathams in 1933) were originally one people, Polynesians, sharing a common ancestry, speaking dialects of the same language, and coming perhaps from the very same group of South Pacific islands hundreds of miles away to the north.

Some probably went direct from those islands to the Chathams, which thus became the landfall for one of the lesser Polynesian migrations — either planned or haphazard. Their legendary pioneer was the great navigator Rongomai, a contemporary of Kupe. Others undoubtedly crossed over from the New Zealand mainland.

But conditions of life on the Chathams were different from those on the main New Zealand islands; so, over the centuries, a different culture developed. In fact, so many differences were noticed by the first Europeans when they arrived towards the end of the eighteenth century, that the people of the Chathams were thought to be of an entirely different race — hence the various theories which arose to account for their presence there.

One great difference was in the way they made their homes. The Maoris, of course, built substantial timbered dwellings (called *whares*) in *pas* or *kaingas* (villages) which they regarded as the permanent residence of their *hapu*, or tribal group. But such was the nature of the Morioris' food-supply — they lived mainly by hunting and fishing — that their way of life was largely nomadic.

So, like nomads everywhere, their homes tended to be light, and quickly constructed. Often enough they were just crude huts or shelters made from the branches of trees. And sometimes their temporary habitations were simple "bowers" or open spaces among the islands' profuse groves of karaka trees whose leafy branches interlocked overhead to make a "ceiling".

Today among the remaining karaka groves in the Chathams one can still see evidence — in the form of vast shell-heaps or middens — of their use as human habitations. In some there are signs that the Moriori scarped or bent the young living trees so that they would grow to give more shelter. Most fascinating evidence of all, however, is the treasury which these groves provide of that unique art form which the Moriori developed, using as their medium the living bark of the karaka tree.

Into this bark their craftsmen incised a fantastic range and number of dendroglyphs (tree-carvings) the full story of which still awaits telling to the outside world. The first substantial study of these carvings was that made in 1947 and 1948 by a lone woman investigator, Miss Christine Jefferson, encouraged by the then Acting Director of the Canterbury Museum, Dr Roger Duff.

To gather information and make copies of the glyphs Miss Jefferson spent just over nine months at the Chathams, in the course of which she rode over 1,000 miles on horseback, walked countless more miles, and slept for seventy-seven nights alone in outback huts. "After long days in the open, days all lovely with sunshine, shadow and living things; after much trial and much tribulation," Miss Jefferson wrote in *The Journal of the*

Many New Zealand schools and colleges foster the arts of the Maori. Sometimes, as in this picture, Pakeha motifs are introduced, the result usually being an attractive fusion of the two cultures.

Reconstruction of *Dinornis maximus*, largest of the thirty-odd species of moa which once roved New Zealand in great droves, feeding on native tussock, twigs, leaves and roots.

The kea, amusing and mischievous, is the practical joker of the bird world.

The tuatara, a living fossil. While resembling, a lizard and often wrongly called one, the tuatara stands alone in the animal world.

Polynesian Society, December 1955, "after being stirred again and again by the discovery of carvings ever more astonishing, more outlandish, and wholly unexpected, I arrived back in New Zealand with some sixty photographs, over two hundred finished drawings of the glyphs, and copious notes."

The bark of the karaka tree is thick, soft but crisp, and easily cut with the Moriori's stone adze, or *toki*, which was from six to twelve inches long. In the carvings, both v-shaped and semi-circular cuts were used, with the main lines incised to depths of from one-quarter to three-quarters of an inch. Different methods of carving were employed, and in many examples the bark within the main lines has been scraped to varying depths to indicate shadow.

Some carvings show a raised or "intaglio" effect as in bas relief or cameos; others have their surfaces contoured, to represent, for example, the human cheek. Of the 259 glyphs which Miss Jefferson studied, 204 were representations of the human figure. Other broad groups into which the carvings fall are (a) zoomorphic representations — mainly birds and fish; (b) trees; (c) weapons and other fashioned objects; (d) rectilinear designs.

Most of the heads are heart-shaped, with pointed chins and a well-defined V (representing the nose) separating the eyes. The faces show surprise, delight, complacency and other human emotions. Usually there are clear distinctions between male and female figures, while activities such as childbirth, hunting and so on are depicted.

Some of the figures are headless, or anthropomorphic. Others have their faces blank. Many are what one islander described as *whakapohoho*, meaning that they have a certain commemorative significance, as with the carved ancestral figures in Maori guest houses.

But whatever the reason for the execution of these carvings, or how the Moriori may have used them in their daily lives, the fact remains that they are now the fast-diminishing remnants of a rare and highly distinctive art form, vulnerable to such agents as weathering, and the inroads of a newer culture. They are quite without any form of legal or other protection.

CHAPTER FIVE

Birds Without Wings

NEW ZEALAND has no native land mammals except for two rare species of bat, which may be indigenous but which are believed by some authorities to have been self-introduced from Australia. This lack of mammals is compensated for by a great wealth and variety of native birds, all vastly interesting, many of them unique.

These birds inhabit all types of terrain and, as the naturalist James Drummond observed: "Some can fly great distances without resting, and others cannot fly at all. Some eat meat, some vegetables, and some anything they can get. Some work all day and sleep all night; others work all night and sleep all day. Some are honest, amiable and obliging, and some are arrant knaves and vagabonds, insatiable gluttons and detestable bullies. Some laugh, others scream and others again sing some of the sweetest songs ever heard on earth." (*Native in New Zealand*; Whitcombe & Tombs Ltd.)

The Kiwi

Quite the most remarkable bird now living is the kiwi, which New Zealand has adopted as one of its national emblems. New Zealand soldiers in the last World War were nicknamed Kiwis, and New Zealanders are called by this name in many countries. One has wryly described his namesake as "a bird which can't see, can't hear, can't think, can't fight . . . but boy can it run!"

Actually not many New Zealanders have ever seen a kiwi in its natural habitat, and even fewer have heard its cry. For this is a nocturnal creature, which sleeps all day in hollow logs and under the roots of trees in the depths of forests — except for some few which live in zoos and other sanctuaries. At night the kiwi stirs itself and snuffles around, seeking food — worms, which it digs out of the ground; insects, berries; and grubs from rotten logs, which it locates by prodding.

Its long slightly curved bill is well adapted for this, as are its nostrils which, unlike those of any other bird, are placed close together at the tip. This enables the kiwi to detect its quarry without the use of sight. At the upper end of the kiwi's beak is a cluster of hairs, for all the world like a cat's whiskers, which are thought to act as antennae, enabling the bird to pick up sound waves caused by the movement of the small creatures it hunts.

With no tail, virtually no wings, and an abnormally long beak, the kiwi certainly is the strangest-looking bird. Even its feathers are abnormal, being for the most part long and hairlike. Roughly the size of a barnyard fowl, the kiwi lays an egg eight times larger than a hen's — weighing about one pound. The bird itself weighs only about four pounds, on average, and this extraordinary disproportion between the hen and the egg is regarded as evidence that, in the course of evolution, the kiwi has become much smaller than its ancestors. Just what those ancestors were, and where they came from, is still a major mystery.

Present classification puts it in the order *Apterygiformes*, indicating a relationship to the ostrich of South Africa, the rhea of South America, the New Zealand moa, the Australian emu, and the cassowary of Australia and New Guinea. These are all ratite birds whose breastbones are raft-like (which the term "ratite" means) and not keeled like those of flying species. Some naturalists think that the kiwi's ancestors may have walked to New Zealand when that country had land links with Australia, South Africa, and South America. Others consider that its ancestors could fly.

Kiwi feathers are long, and hairlike, usually greyish or reddish-brown. They were much prized by the oldtime Maori, who wove them into cloaks of the highest quality to be worn by chieftains. The composition of this bird has been described as a caricature, its odd-shaped body representing no fewer than three distinct bird types; for it has the same head and bill as the long-toed waders, the sturdy legs and clawed feet of the gallinaceous birds (to which our domestic fowl belongs) and the body of the struthiones.

The kiwi has no tail, only the vestige of wings, and no powers of flight; for, since it had no ground foes until man arrived — except perhaps the moa, which it could evade by running or hiding — there was simply no need to fly. Even after the advent of human beings, the kiwi's speed, and its nocturnal way of life deep in the forest, ensured its survival. The coming of the European, however, with his dogs, his firearms, and his destruction of the protecting forests, spelled the kiwi's doom, and its numbers have greatly diminished. Like most other New Zealand native birds it is now closely protected.

The female kiwi, after laying her enormous egg (sometimes two, or even three) shows no further interest in the project, and the male then takes over. He performs the duties of hatching, by sitting on the egg, throughout an abnormal incubation period lasting about seventy-five days, and continues his ministrations until the chick can forage for itself. Another strange trait ascribed to the kiwi is that it drinks water only when feeling unwell — very much like some human beings!

While zoos in many countries are keen to acquire specimens, the New Zealand Government rarely permits a kiwi to leave the country: and only five zoos, those at Auckland, Wellington, London, Edinburgh and San Diego, are known to have kept live kiwis. A number have been reared, however, at the Hawke's Bay Acclimatisation Society's Game Farm near Napier, New Zealand.

The Moa

Linked ancestrally with the kiwi was the moa (now extinct) which has been described as the largest, heaviest and ugliest bird that ever lived. Although there were many smaller species, this feathered monster often stood twelve feet high, weighing as much as a racehorse, and it could kill a man with one kick from either of its massive legs, or with one strike from its short, powerful beak.

Such was *Dinornis maximus* (Dinornis meaning terrible bird; maximus, biggest), largest of about thirty recognised moa species. This creature ate more grass than a bullock; and moas of various shapes and sizes once roamed the country in great droves, as proved by the immense number of moa bones — whole drayloads of them — dug up from swamps and sand-dunes in various parts of the country. In both main islands moa remains have been found among the remnants of Maori camps and cooking-fires, showing that some species were hunted and killed for food in comparatively recent times. The very earliest occupants of the country are thought to have subsisted largely on moa meat, hence the name Moa-hunters given them by the archaeologists.

Among the many thousands of moa skeletons and separate bones that have been unearthed and studied, not a single moa wingbone has ever been found. Moreover, the breastbones show no socket or other device for the articulation of wings. The moa was in fact completely wingless, and thus unique in the whole bird kingdom, both past and present.

Because of its size, an abundance of ground level food-stuffs, and the complete absence of natural predators, the moa did not need to fly; and so, for countless centuries before man arrived, this bird was king. In addition to its diet of grass — the coarse tussock which covered plains and uplands in both islands — the moa ate roots, leaves, fruit and twigs. Excavations have produced moa eggs, perfectly preserved, and with neat holes bored in one end, indicating their use by early inhabitants as water-containers. The largest egg discovered measures about ten by seven inches. Moa feathers have also been found but it seems probable that the birds themselves have been extinct for some 200-300 years.

Last reported sighting of a moa was in 1860, when a worker on an outback sheep farm in the South Island's Lake Mana-pouri district came rushing back to the homestead in a great state of excitement shouting that he had seen a live moa across the Waiau River, between New Zealand's "Great Lakes", Te Anau and Manapouri. But this and other reported sightings have not been accepted by scientists, though many well-preserved moa bones have been found in caves in that area.

The Extinct Bird That Wasn't

In the vast rugged Fiordland region another "extinct" bird, the takahe, was dramatically re-discovered in 1948 after it had been thought for half a century to be non-existent.

The takahe, or *Notornis*, is so rare that until 1948 only four specimens had ever been taken. Nor does it seem that any other sightings, either by Maori or pakeha, had ever been made.

The first specimen was captured in 1849 by a party of sealers at Resolution Island near Dusky Sound, after they had noticed in the snow the trail of a large and unknown bird. They followed the footprints with dogs, eventually sighted their quarry and, after a long chase, captured it alive. For several days the sealers kept this bird aboard their schooner, admiring its gay plumage, its bright-red beak and legs. Then they killed and ate it, each crew member partaking of the dainty, which they declared to be delicious! Fortunately they preserved the skin, which is now in the British Museum.

The second specimen, captured by a Maori two years later, is in the Dominion Museum, Wellington. For almost thirty years no other takahe was sighted until in 1879 a rabbiter's dog caught one in this same Fiordland area. The rabbiter promptly killed the bird; but luckily it was noticed by the station manager who preserved the skin. This found its way to the Dresden Museum, from which it disappeared during World War II. The fourth specimen, now in the Dunedin Museum, was also caught by a dog, on the shores of Lake Te Anau, almost twenty years after the third capture. It was rowed for twenty-five miles down the lake to a point from which it could be sent to Invercargill.

On 20 November 1948 Dr G. B. Orbell, of Invercargill, followed a number of clues which led him to a wild tussock-covered valley in the heart of the New Zealand "badlands". He took with him a movie camera and fishnet. After a long and arduous journey to the valley, which is in the Murchison Range, 2,200 feet above Lake Te Anau, Orbell spotted two takahe, a male and a female, which he captured in his net. He took movie pictures of the birds — the first live takahe ever to be photographed — and then released them. He also saw a third one, which quickly disappeared.

Thus it was established that a colony of takahe existed in this region, which was speedily proclaimed by the New Zealand Government to be a bird sanctuary. Intensive scientific investigation followed, and attempts have been made to rear some birds in captivity.

The takahe also is flightless, with a bright plumage of rich blues and greens, and with vivid red beak and feet, the colour of sealing-wax. The young are jet black when first hatched in their nests of mountain tussock, or "snowgrass", and they soon learn to fend for themselves. Takahe feed on seeds and the soft parts of plants, chiefly the Danthonia, or snowgrass. Except for its lack of flight this bird is remarkably like the pukeko, another native of New Zealand, which lives and nests in the raupo swamps of both main islands.

The Kakapo

Once widely distributed over both main islands but now extremely rare, this New Zealand parrot is another bird that has lost the power of flight. It has wings, but uses them only for gliding. Like the kiwi the kakapo leads a nocturnal life, spending its days hiding in holes among rocks or under the roots of forest trees.

In the North Island there have been no recorded sightings of the kakapo since 1906, so it is doubtful if any still survive there. Even in the South Island the kakapo had been seen so rarely in recent years that many people considered this bird to be extinct. In the early 1960s, however, several live specimens were captured, and attempts were made to rear them in captivity.

The kakapo's plumage, of yellow-green-brown combinations irregularly barred with black, provides excellent camouflage in a forest habitat. The kakapo climbs trees to get berries and nectar, and comes down to earth again by gliding. It is also thought to climb up and glide down again just for fun; and in this way it covers distances of up to ninety yards.

The Weka

North, South and Stewart Island each has its own distinct species of weka, a ground bird which can run very fast, cannot fly, and lives a more or less nocturnal life. Captain James Cook noted in his diary that wekas "eat very well in a pye or fricassee"; and this bird provided chicken dinners for many an early-day bushman, settler, or gold-seeker.

With their cheeky and inquisitive ways wekas also provided

both amusement and annoyance, being arrant thieves prone to enter and ransack bush camps, filching oddments and food, and especially attracted to bright objects such as rings and watches.

"More than once," writes Dr M. I. Soper, a noted bird-watcher, "sitting under a dripping tent-fly, a cup of tea in one hand, a slice of toast in the other, and the weka's presence completely forgotten, have I lost the toast to the sudden thieving snatch of a long beak stabbing with rapier rapidity from between my legs."

The weka feeds on worms, grubs, insects, berries, mice, and the fallen eggs or nestlings of other birds. It also eats both the brown and the black rat, which live in the New Zealand forest and are among the worst enemies of nesting birds. Thus the weka earns an oscar as a destroyer of insect pests and vermin, and a preserver of other bird species.

CHAPTER SIX

Other Amazing Birds

The Kea

Probably no bird has aroused so much controversy among scientists and bird-lovers the world over as the New Zealand kea, a native parrot which lives for the most part high up among the South Island mountains. There its home is a vast wasteland of scrub, tussock, and bare shingle screes between forest and snowline — a striking contrast to the natural habitat of most parrots, which live in the sunny tropics.

Although the kea generally lives far from the haunts of man, it is invariably friendly and inquisitive in the presence of human beings, and it loves to show off. It is, in fact, the complete extrovert of the bird world, always acting the clown when it finds it has a human audience.

With its shining olive-green coat, its merry eyes and perky antics, the kea is a great favourite of hikers and mountaineers. Appearing like desert Arabs from nowhere, one or two of them, soon to be joined by a whole squad, will follow the tramper for miles on end, or sidle up alongside, creating endless delight with their amusing tricks and their ridiculous shuffling gait.

This last derives from the kea's short legs and flat feet, each with four toes, paired fore and aft. In walking, the kea places not only its whole foot on the ground, but also the tarsus; thus it drags its tail-feathers and moves with a clumsy waddle — except when hopping, at which it is adept.

The kea loves to supervise mountain campers, and takes a lively interest in all their activities. It will test the strength of ropes and tents, often reducing them to tatters. During the occupants' absence hordes of keas will invade a camp, fossick around among packs, sleeping bags and utensils, ripping, tearing, scattering and dragging until they have created a complete shambles.

Around dawn they congregate on the roofs of mountain huts, incessantly screeching and calling to one another with their loud "kee-a", "kee-a", and making sleep impossible for the luckless occupant. Then, in relays, a dozen or so will slide down the corrugated iron roofs, shrieking with raucous mirth as they roll off at the bottom — only to scramble up again and repeat the process.

So mischievous is the kea that in some parts of the South Island roadside signs warn the traveller of his presence, as though he were some outlaw with a price upon his head. And that, in fact, is what the kea is — not on account of his camp depredations, but because of his "record" as a sheep-killer.

The kea has a strong, scimitar-shaped beak, broad at the base, and tapering to a needle-sharp point; and the bird is accused of using this beak as a weapon for attacks upon sheep. Primarily a vegetarian, feasting throughout past ages upon leaves, shoots and berries, the kea had its curiosity aroused, and began investigating, when pakeha graziers introduced sheep into its high country habitat. Here was a novel source of fun, to be exploited by jumping on to sheeps' backs and clinging by beak and claw while the terrified mounts careered madly around.

Not such good fun for the sheep, of course, which often stampeded in mobs and sometimes fell over cliffs or down steep valleys. Other matters for investigation by the inquisitive kea were "cast" sheep (those fallen to the ground and unable to rise again), others caught in thickets, and even the skins which shepherds hung upon posts or fences. These were explored by pecking and tearing; and so, it is thought, some keas developed a taste for mutton.

Alarmed by what they saw, heard about, or deduced, high country graziers sought to exterminate the kea by paying a bounty for every bird killed; and many a shepherd has been able to double his wages by shooting keas. Today in New Zealand a "kea gun" is a well-recognised weapon, while the kea remains among the very few native birds not protected by law. Many people hold that extermination is a drastic and unnecessary way of dealing with a menace which may be far less serious than is suspected. For while some keas undoubtedly do molest sheep, the vast majority of them are innocent.

Gannets Galore

The gannet or sea goose is certainly not unique to New Zealand, but this country is probably the only place in the world where gannets nest on the mainland. Not everywhere on the mainland, but on just one small narrow strip where, for centuries, thousands upon thousands of these fascinating birds have crowded together in the breeding season.

Such is the world-famous colony at Cape Kidnappers, on the North Island's east coast, named by Captain Cook from an incident which occurred there during his celebrated voyage of discovery in 1769. On that occasion a Tahitian boy named Taieto — a member of Cook's crew — was taken by the Maoris, though he managed to escape by jumping out of his captors' canoe and swimming back to Cook's ship, the *Endeavour*.

Human access to the gannetry is difficult (hence, no doubt, the colony's persistence) and one reaches there today by a five-mile hike from the hamlet of Clifton, which has road access. But before entering the sanctuary the visitor must first obtain a permit from the Commissioner of Crown Lands at Napier (the nearest city) or from the office of the Clifton Domain; for the colony is rigorously protected.

During the breeding season — eggs are laid generally in October or November — one may view the amazing spectacle of a whole broad plateau, 360 feet above the sea, covered with gannets: most of them sitting on their nests; some clumsily leaving; others returning, each to his own home, with uncanny precision. For so numerous are the habitations, and so closely constructed are they that the return of each bird to his own would seem impossible. The homecoming of a nest-owner involves quite a feat of aerobatics, since the adult's wing-span is about five feet, while the nest is usually less than two feet wide.

Yet it happens. And "constructed" is hardly the word, for these gannet nests are no more than crude mounds of seaweed, piled up on the guano and garbage of previous years' habitations. In each nest the female lays one large, thick-shelled egg, about the size of a turkey's, and the parents take turns at hatching. For this they hold the egg between their webbed feet. Incubation takes about six and a half weeks.

Finally there emerges an ungainly chick, bare, black, blind and ugly. But in less than ten days the fledgling has grown into a charming little creature rather like a duckling, covered all over with thick white down. In ten months this fluff has changed to a dark, mottled greyish-brown plumage, and the young bird is then ready to float or fly. At this stage the New Zealand gannets migrate to eastern Australia, returning to breed in their fourth year.

The Tui

While most New Zealand birds mentioned so far can neither fly nor sing, the tui is adept at both. It is, in fact, among the world's most brilliant songsters, with an extraordinary clarity of tone, range of notes, and vocal versatility. Its song is often the first to be heard in the New Zealand forest in the morning and the last at night. Tuis are also accomplished mimics, and the oldtime Maoris often kept them as pets, teaching them to talk and to lure other birds — destined for the oven — by imitating their songs.

Rather larger than the European blackbird, the tui has a shining plumage, predominantly bluish and greenish black. Silver-grey filaments ornament the neck, while at the throat is a dangling double-tuft of white curved feathers, suggestive of a cleric's collar; so the tui is often called the "parson bird".

The tui is a great favourite in New Zealand where it is often seen and heard around country homesteads, on the fringes of forests, and in those city parks, schools and suburbs which grow nectar-bearing trees and shrubs. Having strong powers of flight, the tui frequents high treetops, foraging there for berries and insects, and for the nectar of flowers, especially the rata, the kowhai, the puriri and the pohutukawa. It extracts the nectar with its remarkable brush-tipped tongue, and in doing so it gathers pollen on its head-feathers. Thus the tui pollinates a number of native trees and shrubs. Other points of interest are the bird's noisy, undulating flight, and its fondness for aerobatics, which it performs while pursuing winged insects.

As a consumer of insects, and with no propensity for raiding planted crops or orchards, the tui rates as a friend of man, and is protected by law. Since it lives for the most part high above the ground, this bird is less vulnerable than many others to introduced enemies such as dogs, rats, stoats and weasels. It is widely admired for its beautiful plumage, happy singing, speed of movement, and general air of bustle and gaiety. Thus the tui's survival seems assured.

The Bellbird

This elegant songster, with its shapely body, long tail and curved beak, is another New Zealand favourite which, after some setbacks, is now adapting to European settlement. Its melodies are as rich and varied as the tui's, the notes resembling a peal of small bells.

The bellbird still adds to the brilliant dawn chorus which delights sojourners in the New Zealand bush — though its admirers are often deceived by the mischievous tui, which can mimic almost to perfection the songs of its rival. Unique to the bellbird, however, are a number of distinctive flutelike notes, which ring out as a peal of chimes.

The bellbird, like the tui, subsists on insects, berries and nectar. Both the male and the female help to build the nest, in which three or four eggs are laid and the parents continue to feed their young for about ten days after they leave their nests.

The Kotuku, or White Heron

This bird is so rare in New Zealand that it has only one known nesting-place there — on the banks of the Waitangiroto Stream near Okarito in Westland. About twenty pairs nest in this place annually, on crude platforms of sticks, which often overhang the water.

Known locally as the "white heron", this bird is actually an egret, as remarkable for the beauty of its snow-white plumage as for the rarity of its appearances in any one part of the country, though its range extends from Parengarenge in the far north to Stewart Island, and sometimes even further south to the sub-Antarctic islands. Although Maori legend features the kotuku as the embodiment of rarity, grace and beauty, and as a frequenter of the spirit world, this bird is a comparative newcomer to New Zealand. The colony there was established by birds wind-blown from eastern Australia, which has large numbers.

After the breeding season, the kotuku disperse singly or in pairs to the furthest parts of the country. There they forage, usually alone, in swamps, lagoons, or the shallower coastal waters. They eat small fish, including eels, which they capture by standing perfectly still until the prey swims within striking distance. Some have been seen to capture small birds, swallowing them head first, feathers and all. Others sometimes rob shags of their catch as they come to the surface.

Standing about three feet high, this bird is so solitary in its habits, and so sparse in its dispersal in New Zealand, that Maori lore credits the kotuku as being seen only once in the lifetime of any man.

The Rough-faced Shag

Even rarer than the kotuku is New Zealand's rough-faced or carunculated shag, of which probably less than 100 exist anywhere. Unlike the kotuku, which came from Australia, the rough-faced shag has only one breeding-place in the whole world — a few rocky islets in the Marlborough Sounds, where it was first discovered in 1773 by the naturalist Forster during Captain Cook's second voyage.

Known locally as the "king" shag because of its size and colouring this bird never travels far from its breeding ground, being sedentary in habit and not a strong flier — though like all other shags it can swim and dive well.

During a breeding season, which extends over several months, the female lays three or four elliptical eggs, pale blue in colour, in a solid circular nest made of sticks and seaweed cemented together with guano.

The Fantail

Best-loved of all New Zealand birds is the dainty little fantail, called by the Maoris *piwakawaka*. Friendly, fearless, and always cheerful, this bewitching creature, with plump body about the size of a pullet's egg, flirts its fascinating fan in a variety of situations.

The fantail's natural habitat is in the open outer spaces of forest and scrubland, where it pursues small flying insects such as gnats, sandflies and midges. In so doing it performs enchanting aerobatics, darting, turning and twisting with amazing agility.

Since human settlements tend to increase rather than diminish its food supply, the fantail has been able to live amicably with man, making itself at home in gardens, shrubberies and shelterbelts. It will fly quite close to people and even perch upon them. Sometimes fantails fly through open doors or windows, right inside houses, schools and other occupied buildings, hunting houseflies around ceilings and windows and chirping cheerily all the time.

Fantails begin nesting in August, when both parents set about the business of home-building. The hen lays three pale cream-coloured eggs, lightly speckled with greyish-brown.

The Godwits

To describe here all the fascinating birds of New Zealand would be impossible; but a passing bow must be made to a few more, for example the godwits which, seeking eternal summer, spend part of their lives in flight between New Zealand and the Arctic tundras of Siberia and Alaska, where they breed.

Of moderate size, with long legs and long upcurved bills, the godwits are waders, like the great majority of New Zealand migrant birds. They arrive in this country during the latter half of September (early spring) and for about six months they populate sand and mudflats along many parts of the coast. Flocks numbering several hundreds are then a common sight.

When autumn comes, the godwits move northward in New Zealand, and finally congregate on a number of beaches, ready for their long return journey to the Arctic. This they make via chains of islands in the western Pacific. One noted point of departure is Spirits Bay, at the farthest end of the North Island. According to Maori tradition, Spirits Bay was also the taking-off place for the souls of the dead, which slid down into the water from the branches of a huge pohutukawa tree still to be seen growing at Spirits Bay.

The Wrybill

No one knows what evolutionary quirk first induced the plump little New Zealand wrybill plover to eat from the side of its mouth; but whatever may have started it, the trend has continued, and today this plover's bill grows with a definite twist to the right, making it unique among all birds. Others may flaunt their down-turned, up-turned, or even crossed mandibles; but only the New Zealand wrybill boasts this sideways deflection, noticeable even in the unborn chick.

Found only on the two main islands of New Zealand the wrybill follows a curious migratory pattern. In August it flocks to its only known breeding ground — a series of shingly riverbeds on the eastern side of the South Island, between southern Marlborough and northern Otago. There it makes a perfunctory scrape in the sand before laying its pair of greyish-green, minutely-speckled eggs. These, and the bird itself, blend in perfectly with the surrounding stones and shingle.

Between December and May the wrybills migrate northwards to winter on beaches and mudflats in the Auckland Province; and while some travel almost to the North Cape, large numbers can be seen on seashores quite close to Auckland City. This diminutive wader, standing only seven or eight inches high, has such confidence in its natural camouflage that whole flocks will often stand, motionless and unobserved, until some intruder comes within a few feet of them. Then they rise in a body and wheel overhead in graceful flight, flashing white and silver against the sky.

The Rifleman

Just as New Zealand once harboured the world's largest bird it now has one of the world's smallest — the rifleman, or New Zealand wren, called *titi-pounamu* by the Maori. Only three inches from bill-tip to the end of its stumpy tail the rifleman inhabits the forests of both main islands, especially the South Island beech forests, which provide an abundance of the spiders and insects on which it feeds.

While the rifleman is considerably larger than many of the humming birds, which resemble bumble bees, it is smaller than

Trout fishing at Ohinemutu, Rotorua.

A helicopter recovering venison from rugged mountain country. Often the live deer are picked off by a sharp shooter sitting in the helicopter.

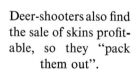

Deer-shooters also find the sale of skins profitable, so they "pack them out".

some species, e.g. those which live high up in the Andes Mountains and grow to a length of five or six inches. Watchers are intrigued by the activity of this tiny fellow — the smallest of all New Zealand birds — as it runs up tree trunks in search of its food. Having only limited powers of flight the rifleman rarely pursues flying insects.

The name derives from a fancied resemblance of this bird's plumage to the uniform of one of the early New Zealand rifle regiments. Unlike the humming birds, of which there are 320 species, the rifleman belongs to a most exclusive family, for the New Zealand wrens comprise only four species, one of which is extinct.

CHAPTER SEVEN

Strange Creatures

The Tuatara

Resembling a large lizard, and often called one, New Zealand's tuatara does not belong to any of the known lizard families. It stands quite alone in the animal world — a "living fossil" — sole survivor of the Rhynchocephalia, saurians of the Mesozoic era once widespread throughout the world. All species except the tuatara became extinct more than 100 million years ago.

Only in New Zealand has this order survived, and even there its unique representative, the tuatara, is extremely rare. No longer can this "little dragon" be found on the mainland, where it once lived in considerable numbers. It exists only on some fifteen or sixteen small islands around the coast.

There it is closely protected, and access to its habitations is difficult. So to see a live tuatara today most people must go to a city zoo. Zoos in other countries have requested specimens, but few have been sent. Only one pair of tuataras — male with female — has ever been exported, and those went to Gerald Durrell's famous Jersey Zoological Park in the Channel Islands, with the idea of breeding the creatures in captivity, and thus perhaps regenerating stocks in New Zealand.

Adult tuataras are about two feet long, but when first hatched the young measure less than four inches. They emerge from tough-skinned drab-white oval eggs about the size of ping-pong balls. During the months October to December, the female lays a batch of a dozen or so, in a hollow some four or five inches deep which she scoops out of loose soil. Having laid the eggs she covers them over and then abandons them. Incubation takes from thirteen to fourteen months, the embryo developing very quickly at first (during the New Zealand summer) then slowing down, or "hibernating" during the winter — a rare phenomenon.

Though not vicious as a rule, tuataras have been known to nip one another, and even to bite with their three rows of strong teeth people intent on handling them. The teeth do not grow separately in sockets, like the teeth of fish or mammals, but are actually serrations of the jawbone covered with enamel-like substance. The tuatara's claws, too, are sharp and formidable, so catching a live specimen can be painful to the unwary.

Once or twice a year the adult tuatara sheds its old skin and grows a bright new one, olive-green with reddish patches and many spots of a whitish lemon colour. This skin soon changes to a dull uniform brown which provides adequate camouflage. The adult has a large head, a tail which can be regrown if severed, and a heavy body supported by short legs. Yet the tuatara is not sluggish as is often supposed, but surprisingly quick, sometimes taking cover in a flash after remaining motionless perhaps for hours. The scientific name, *Sphaenodon punctatus*, derives from the large wedge-shaped front teeth of the upper jaw (Sphaenodon) and the many light-coloured spots on the skin (punctatus).

A prominent feature of the tuatara is a ridge of spines, or skin-folds, along its back and head, which the creature erects when excited. Though formidable in appearance these folds are entirely harmless, being soft and flexible. It also has a third (or "pineal") eye in the top of its head, as do some lizards and primitive fishes, but this organ in the tuatara has no sight function. It is very small — only about one-fiftieth of an inch in diameter — and is covered by scales and skin. In newly-hatched tuataras the position of this "third eye" is marked by an area of transparent scale. The two normal eyes of the tuatara have vertical pupils.

Other peculiarities include the absence of ear openings, and the absence of any penis or copulatory organ in the male, thus making the tuatara unique among living reptiles and placing it apart from the snakes and lizards, which have two such organs.

Tuataras are reputed to live for 200 years or longer; but research on this question has only recently begun. Today their main habitat is the rocky Stephens Island in Cook Strait. There, as elsewhere, they often share the burrows of petrels (seabirds), a strange partnership but usually an amicable one — though adult petrels have been found in some burrows with their heads bitten off, and no doubt petrel chicks sometimes supplement the tuatara's normal diet of insects, snails, small lizards, and beetles.

A Pondless Frog

Both layman and scientist marvel at this unique New Zealand frog; for, living as it does in a virtually waterless habitat, the *Leiopelma* has no access to pond, pool or stream in which its offspring can enjoy a happy active life as free-swimming tadpoles. And so it has evolved its own special mode of larval development.

The *Leiopelma* does not skip the tadpole stage, but develops it within the egg, in a gelatinous capsule filled with water . . . a pond-substitute. Here the embryo completes all the usual frog-development stages and is even able to move about while inside the capsule. In due course it emerges as a complete adult.

First to discover the New Zealand frog was an army surgeon, Arthur Saunders Thomson, who, while watching some gold-diggers near Coromandel in 1852, saw one captured from under a boulder. This specimen was shown to many Maoris, but no one could name it, and none had ever seen such a creature before. In 1858 the Austrian scientist, Ferdinand von Hochstetter, collected a few specimens from the Coromandel Peninsula, and the frog was subsequently named in his honour *Leiopelma hochstetteri*.

Another species, *L. hamiltoni*, has been called the "Stephens Island frog" because its main habitat is that same steep 500-acre island in Cook Strait where most of the tuataras now live. There, 1000 feet up, on a stark boulder-bank only eighty yards long by sixty yards wide, it works out its extraordinary life pattern. For its only source of water there is rain, mist and dew — no pond, no river, scarcely ever a trickle.

In 1958 Dr Elsie Stephenson identified another small colony of *L. hamiltoni* living under different, but equally unlikely, conditions on Maud Island, in Pelorus Sound. A third species, *L. archeyi*, has been named after Sir Gilbert Archey, formerly Director of the Auckland Institute and War Memorial Museum.

Its habitat is high up in the Coromandel Range, east of Auckland.

All three species are closely protected by law, and no one who discovers a native frog should handle it or disturb its hiding place, for these interesting creatures, rarer than the tuatara, soon die if exposed to wind, sun or dry air.

A Carnivorous Snail

As every gardener knows, snails are ardent vegetarians; but New Zealand has a meat-eating species which lives on worms and slugs. This is the so-called kauri snail, named *pupurangi* by the Maori, and by the naturalist *Paryphanta busbyi*.

This snail does not haunt the kauri forests, as one might suppose, but it shares the same geographical distribution. Observers have watched one demolishing an eight-inch worm, the method being to suffocate the quarry before eating, by dragging it inside the shell. A really ambitious *Paryphanta* will sometimes take on two or three worms at a time.

Another unusual thing about the kauri snail is that it lays eggs similar in shape and outward appearance to those of a bird — hard shell and all, about the size of a small pea.

Marine Oddities

Cook Strait, separating New Zealand's North and South Islands, has an undersea canyon which plunges precipitously from near the Wellington shoreline to a depth of over 6,000 feet — more than a mile. This canyon connects with the vast "deeps" of the Pacific Ocean, and comprises an unexplored blackland intriguing to scientists and to commercial fishermen.

Currents swirling through Cook Strait sometimes propel the denizens of this canyon up into shallower waters, where from time to time they are captured in the nets of trawlers, or washed up on to beaches. Such creatures, conditioned to exist in total darkness and to withstand pressures of more than a ton to the square inch, have little chance of survival in the sea's upper regions, so a scientific study of marine life in this canyon is extremely difficult.

Nevertheless it was initiated a few years ago by Professor L. R. Richardson (a Canadian) who was then head of the

Department of Zoology at Victoria University, Wellington. He was assisted in his investigations by a devoted band of scientists and students who gave up their holidays and week-ends, and by the crews and skippers of local fishing boats.

One of their first projects was to build a mammoth mouse-trap, in an effort to catch live specimens of the decapod or giant squid — a fearsome, almost mythical, deep-sea creature with eyes the size of dinner-plates, a ten-foot-long body, and ten cupped tentacles each measuring up to twenty-five feet.

The legends of all seafaring nations, including the Maori, have stories of sea monsters with many arms which lurk in gloomy ocean depths where they battle with the mighty sperm whale. They are depicted on Mycenean urns, Japanese colour prints and woodcuts, ancient European stained glass windows. But until comparatively recent times these creatures were not accepted scientifically, and very little is known about them.

A member of the mollusc family, the giant squid is thus related to the octopus, to small shellfish such as the cockle and the oyster, and to the garden snail. Jet-propelled, it travels backwards at great speed, sucking water into a hollow mantle which surrounds its body, and then ejecting it from a siphon under the head.

To quote Professor Richardson, when interviewed by the Wellington *Evening Post:* "In the centre of their ten tentacles is their mouth, equipped with a sharp beak, remarkably similar to that of a parrot. Each of the suckers — their tentacles carry hundreds — has a bony skeleton which projects into the flesh of their prey or enemies. Sixty-foot sperm whales, and large porpoises, wear for years the scars of these large circular suckers in the flesh of their head and throat."

But although these creatures have been noticed swimming on the surface near the Chatham Islands, and a number have been washed ashore on beaches near Wellington, none has yet been captured in Cook Strait.

Besides these giants, and other grotesque creatures, the Strait has a species of shrimp which is found nowhere else except in the Atlantic Ocean, at depths between 1,800 and 9,000 feet. This New Zealand type lives a mere sixty feet down. Also in Cook Strait (again to quote Richardson) is a snipe eel "poking about at a ridiculous fifty fathoms" while all its known relatives inhabit the world's deepest oceans, at depths of at least 1,000 fathoms.

Cook Strait trawlers have retrieved (sometimes from the stomachs of giant cod) odd specimens of the rarely-seen angler fish, a "swimming stomach" which lurks at depths of up to 9,000 feet, and is able to swallow and digest other fish larger than itself. Its name derives from a slender rod projecting from the creature's head, with a luminous red bulb at the end which attracts other fish and brings them within reach of its mouth. Inky black in colour, the angler has two tiny eyes. But they are of doubtful use in the blacked-out depths which it inhabits.

Other weird creatures taken from Cook Strait include blood-red prawns and shrimps, the latter more than seven inches long; crimson and purple squids; and a deep-water dogfish — green-eyed, shovel-nosed, and covered with fur. Most shocking is the blind electric ray, or numbfish, with two "blow-holes" instead of eyes, and a built-in generator which creates enough ohms to knock a man back.

CHAPTER EIGHT

Fishing, Hunting, Shooting

An Angler's Paradise

Zane Grey named New Zealand the "Angler's El Dorado", and sportsmen everywhere agree that the fishing there is easily the world's best.

New Zealand is a country of rivers, lakes and streams, practically all of which are well-stocked with brown and rainbow trout, many with salmon, and a few with fontinalis, the American brook trout.

Fishing is never more than a few miles away, via first-class highways, and it is virtually free. Licences are cheap, bag limits generous. On Taupo, New Zealand's largest lake, the limit is at present twenty fish per day. At Lake Rotorua, in the heart of the thermal region, a fisherman may take as many brown trout as he can capture, while the bag limit for rainbow is eight fish per day.

These lakes, both of which are in the North Island, and easily accessible from Auckland and Wellington, may be fished throughout the year. In the trout-rich Rotorua area, except for a few streams, the season extends from the beginning of October to the end of June. Elsewhere in New Zealand it generally begins in October and ends in April.

The scope allowed to anglers at Taupo and Rotorua stems from the fact that there are, actually, *too many* trout there even though several hundred tons are taken annually from Taupo alone. Years back, twenty-pounders were quite common, and the average weight of captured rainbows was ten and a half pounds. But an increase in numbers has depleted the food supply, so, despite corrective measures such as netting, today's average weight of the Taupo rainbow is about four pounds, and the average length twenty inches. Averages for brown trout stand now at around six pounds and twenty-four inches.

Both brown and rainbow trout are introduced species — the former from England via Tasmania, where it first arrived after extraordinary vicissitudes on 21 April 1864 in the form of ova. By the end of May that year some 300 troutlings had hatched in the Tasmanian breeding ponds; and when they first spawned, in the winter of 1866, ova were offered to the Canterbury Acclimatisation Society.

But at that time the Society's ponds were not ready. In August of the following year, however, 800 ova were sent to New Zealand — half of them for Canterbury and the other half for Otago. Only three out of all these survived; and even those three, after hatching, were lost in a flood which overwhelmed the Canterbury hatcheries at Hagley Park, Christchurch.

But now comes the most fantastic bit of all: two of these three were actually recaptured, and they proved to be a male and a female! From their progeny, and that of some of the 300 which survived in Tasmania, the world-famous brown trout fishing resources of New Zealand were built up.

Tailpiece: the male ancestor of this mighty progeny, weighing nine and a quarter pounds when killed, ended his days on a vice-regal platter — that of Sir James Fergusson, then Governor-General of New Zealand.

New Zealand's rainbow trout were introduced from North America in 1883, a first and only shipment of ova resulting in the present vast rainbow population of this country. In the great eel-free expanse of Taupo's 250 square miles these immigrants flourished, and their progeny has since spread, thanks to the efforts of the New Zealand Marine Department, the Internal Affairs Department, and the various Acclimatisation Societies throughout the country.

Taupo, with its 110 miles of shoreline, is the most popular North Island fishing resort. About forty streams flow into the lake, with good fishing at the mouths of twenty. There, at peak times, and in the best places, "anglers stand almost elbow to elbow across the stream-mouths in a line-up known as the 'picket fence'. But if the anglers jostle each other, so, almost, do the trout".

The main Auckland-Wellington highway skirts the eastern

shores of Lake Taupo, along which are numerous hotels, fishing lodges and camping sites available to visitors, besides innumerable private houses and cabins, many of them used as holiday homes by city-dwelling owners. Postal services in the area are good, and there are many general stores where most normal requirements can be met, and fishing gear of all kinds can be hired or purchased. At the northern end of the lake is the fast-growing commercial centre of Taupo with all the facilities of the modern New Zealand city.

New Zealand does not have "private" fishing waters (except for a few Maori reserves) and anglers may go virtually anywhere so long as they observe the normal courtesies of obtaining permission from the landowner to cross his property, and of giving due care to gates, fences, crops and livestock. Any kind of single-hook lure or spoon is permitted on the North Island lakes; and spinning and bait-casting are also permitted in most of them. Trolling is legal if practised 300 yards or more from the mouth of any stream; gaffing is generally illegal, and any trout caught in a lake must be returned to the water if its length is less than fourteen inches. The minimum length for fish taken from streams varies from nine to twelve inches, according to the locality.

Angling in the South Island is even more varied than in the North, and it has in many places the added attraction of enchanting alpine scenery. Brown trout predominate, but rainbow too are plentiful in many of the lakes. All provinces have their well-stocked waters, and in the deep, clear, snow-fed rivers such as the Cleddau and the Clinton the fish show up distinctly against white sandy beds.

Quinnat salmon abound in the rivers of Canterbury, which flow from the mighty Southern Alps across broad, fertile farmlands to the sea. These rivers are easily reached by road and rail — or one may fly — from the large "English" city of Christchurch. Quinnat salmon caught in these rivers usually weigh from twelve to twenty pounds, sometimes from thirty-five to forty pounds. Atlantic salmon thrive in the Waiau River system, close to New Zealand's southern Fiordland, and in the mountain-cradled Lakes Te Anau and Manapouri. Trout fishing licences also hold good for salmon.

Monsters of the Deep

Nowhere on earth has big-game fishing developed as it has done in New Zealand. Elsewhere strong arms, a sea-going stomach and a well-packed wallet are usually required. Here the pursuit and capture of the world's largest species of fish is anybody's sport, not the rare privilege of the tough and well-heeled. No licences are needed, and fish may be taken at any time, though the season usually extends from November to June and the best catches are made from January to March or April.

Game fishing first began to boom in New Zealand in the 1920s. Zane Grey's visit in 1926, and his book which told the world, gave the sport a boost. Local enterprise followed this up by providing many facilities. But nature has played the biggest part by endowing New Zealand with superbly stocked waters within easy distance of the shore, and snug bays and harbours, many of them island-studded, to serve as bases. So it is not surprising that world big game fishing contests have been held in New Zealand.

The main hunting areas all lie within, or just outside, a 300-mile arc which sweeps from Mangonui in the far north to Mayor Island in the Bay of Plenty. This arc passes within seventy miles of Auckland City, a distance spanned by a number of inhabited islands, some of which have regular sea and air services from Auckland.

Small amphibian planes can be chartered in that city, so less than an hour after arriving there your deep-sea fisherman can find himself in business, trolling or drifting right on the big fish grounds. But he may, in the course of a time-restricted visit, venture much further afield; for each of the six main bases for deep-sea angling (Whangaroa, the Bay of Islands, Whangarei, Kawau Island, Mercury Bay, and Tauranga) can be reached in a few hours by surface travel. Another noted rendezvous is Mayor Island, twenty-two miles north of Tauranga. At most of these places specially designed and equipped launches run by experienced fishermen may be hired at reasonable rates, with all the necessary gear included.

As an example of what can be done by short-term visitors, one American tourist on a single-day stopover at Auckland was able to reach Zane Grey's former base at Otehei in the Bay of Islands, land a 320-pound mako shark there, and be back on board his liner by 6 pm, boasting of his achievements.

For the more leisurely angler — a class which now takes in a rapidly-growing number of New Zealanders — the big game available includes blue, black, and striped marlin; mako, thresher, hammerhead, and tiger sharks; yellowtail (kingfish); and tuna. The true swordfish (broadbill) is rare in New Zealand waters, though some weighing over 600 pounds have been caught there. About the only restrictions concern the capture of swordfish and marlin, which must be fished with rod and line (no heavier than No. 39 linen thread) with a limit of four fish taken from one boat in one day.

World records established in New Zealand waters include a thresher shark weighing 922 pounds caught at the Bay of Islands by the British angler W. W. Dowding in 1937; a seasonal tally taken round the eleven-mile coastline of Mayor Island in 1948-49, comprising 788 game fish including twenty-seven sharks and 749 marlin; and a mako shark weighing 1061 pounds landed by New Zealander Jim Penwarden in February 1970. An experienced angler, Mr Penwarden was fishing from the launch *Abalone* two miles north of Mayor Island when he hooked this monster. He fought it for three hours before it was boated, and in the struggle it towed the *Abalone* four miles further out to sea.

Trolling is the most popular method of fishing in New Zealand waters, and more is being done now with light tackle so that the fish are not just slaughtered, but landed as a result of the angler's skill. The main bait used is kahawai, itself a fighting fish with plenty of verve and vigour, and weighing usually from two to four pounds. The kahawai abounds in New Zealand waters and provides preliminary sport of no mean order, especially when angled on extra-light gear.

With Dog and Gun

Since its first settlement by Europeans, New Zealand has seen the introduction of over 130 species of birds, some forty fish species, and more than fifty species of mammals; but only about one quarter of the birds and fish, and three-fifths of the mammals have become firmly established.

The motive at first was to build up food supplies, since much of the land, being heavily forested, was not immediately suitable for cropping, and there were no indigenous meat-producing animals. Then, in the 1860s and 1870s, as farming and settlement got under way, acclimatisation societies were formed up and down the country to introduce fauna not only for eating, but for sentimental reasons and for sport.

So today New Zealand provides excellent game shooting, particularly of waterfowl which are in good numbers throughout the country. Good upland game shooting is also available in localised areas. The season opens early in May (about the beginning of the New Zealand winter) and each April New Zealand's Minister of Internal Affairs gazettes regulations which proclaim the opening and closing dates for shooting in the different areas, together with bag limits and other restrictions which apply for the approaching season.

Most New Zealand shooters use trained dogs, pointers and retrievers, which are virtually indispensable. This puts the visitor at a disadvantage, since the admission of any kind of dog to New Zealand is severely restricted, and it is not always easy to hire, borrow or buy well-trained animals. The best plan, probably, would be for the visiting sportsman to contact local shooters, who are usually only too happy to include overseas enthusiasts in their shooting parties.

Stalking and Trapping

The taking of red deer and certain other four-footed game in New Zealand has practically no limits, other than the skill and endurance of the hunter, and of his quarry. It is widely conceded that New Zealand provides the best deer stalking — and the cheapest — in the world. Not only is this sport readily available without fees, bag limits, or closed seasons to anyone who cares to pursue it, but many New Zealanders now earn their living as deer-hunters — an occupation with a bonus instead of a penalty on the number of animals slain.

Contrast this with the United States, where deer are closely protected, and during the short hunting season there is a limit of one beast for each hunter; or with Canada, where in the province of British Columbia, non-residents hunting big game must with a few exceptions be accompanied by a licensed British Columbia guide, and, on completion of the hunt, have the guide endorse their licenses. In New Zealand the hunter needs neither guide nor license, and he may hunt round the clock from January to December, entirely on his own. Although it is inadvisable for the independent hunter to choose his own territory (he may not, for example, shoot where Government hunters are operating) a suitable area is always available, and he can usually find someone who will lead him to the more favourable places. Such a guide might be some keen and knowledgeable local, of purely amateur status, a ranger, or the paid employee of one of the many commercial enterprises which now provide deer-hunting "safaris".

The first red deer were introduced to New Zealand in the 1850s by early British settlers, nostalgic for "home" conditions. Rabbits, too, were introduced for similar reasons, for food, for sport, and for the value of their pelts, as early as 1838. A number of other imported animals failed to become acclimatised and soon died out; but others found conditions so much to their liking that they multiplied enormously, and over-ran large tracts of country. And, since they no longer served man's interests but conflicted actively with them, some animal species such as the rabbit, the opossum and the red and the fallow deer were classed officially as "vermin" or pests. A price was put upon their heads, tails, ears, claws or such other parts nominated from time to time as tokens of their destruction. And so today in New Zealand we find men earning their living as professional deer cullers or shooters usually employed by the Government, while a recently developed export trade in venison allows the use of helicopters and other modern devices for the extermination of these animals.

Other deer species which have survived in sufficient numbers to provide good sport include the Virginian, Japanese, moose (elk) and sambar. In the Fiordland region there are also wapiti (Canadian stag) descended from animals presented to the New Zealand nation in 1905 by President Theodore Roosevelt, and others purchased in America at the same time. Only eighteen of the twenty wapiti thus acquired were alive on reaching New Zealand, but their descendants have since multiplied and spread over a wide area. Nowhere else in the Southern Hemisphere do wapiti live in the wild state; and this New Zealand herd interbreeds with red deer to produce a unique hybrid — one, moreover, which is fertile.

Other game animals of distinguished origin are chamois — the small, south-European antelope — first sent to New Zealand by the Emperor Franz Josef from his hunting estates in Austria. These, and Himalayan tahr (sometimes spelled thar) now abound in the South Island alpine regions. Tahr, as every sportsman knows, are agile creatures like outsized goats, standing over three feet high and weighing up to 200 pounds. They provide fine sport for the hardy hunter, who in New Zealand must be prepared to encounter rugged country and live under primitive conditions.

Most amateur hunters belong to the New Zealand Deer Stalkers' Association, which has numerous branches in both islands. Professional hunters often "go bush" in lonely camps or huts for six months at a stretch. They work in steep country of up to 6,000 feet where supplies are flown in by plane and dropped by parachute.

One way and another, more than 150,000 deer are killed each year in New Zealand, and some of this killing has been likened to the nineteenth-century buffalo hunts of North America where thousands of the animals were slaughtered by driving frenzied herds past hunters' ambushes. But here the herders mount helicopters, not horses. At first "choppers" carrying three or four sharp-shooters with high-powered rifles would locate scattered herds in remote plains and mountain valleys. The deer flocked together in bewildered mobs, the 'copter touched down, and the shooters leapt out. In no time twenty animals lay dead on the ground. A day's bag for one machine ranged from about 100 to 150.

Latterly, this method has been replaced by shooting direct from the helicopter — also used for freighting out the gutted and beheaded carcasses. From landing grounds at Queenstown and other centres venison is conveyed to freezing and processing plants before being shipped overseas.

Other Game

Hunting wild pigs with specially trained dogs is another thrilling sport for hardy types, especially in the forested mountain country common to both main islands. Undeterred by vicious attacks from ripping tusks, the dogs corner their quarry in a restricted space, and hold on grimly until the hunter moves in to knife the savagely fighting animal.

Wild pigs in New Zealand are called "Captain Cookers" because they are thought to be descendants of animals released, as a meat supply for the Maoris, by the great navigator. But many of the wild pigs which now infest the forests have sprung from domestic stock imported more recently for the development of the nation's economy. Throughout the years, numbers of these "tame" pigs have escaped from captivity and "gone bush", seeking more amenable porcine haunts. Conditions in the wild have favoured the pigs, which today often ravage farm crops and kill and eat young lambs. Their destruction therefore is encouraged.

Eradication policies now operating in New Zealand, and the national hostility shown towards certain species of animals, are often misunderstood by people who live elsewhere; and so it should be explained, perhaps, that the cause does not lie in any widespread spirit of sadism or savagery, but actually in a grim battle for survival which still goes on in this country. New Zealanders exist mainly on the products of their pastures and forests, which they work hard to develop. But two-thirds of the country is either hilly or mountainous; and so the conservation of forest cover on hilltops and steep slopes is essential to arrest the loss caused by slips, floods and erosion, which take an annual toll of millions of tons of precious soil.

Highly destructive to these protective forests (both native and planted) and to the commercial ones, are wild goats, deer and opossums — the last-named being similar to but different from the American opossum. It is, in fact, a native of Australia, introduced to New Zealand between 1858 and 1920, and once highly protected because of the commercial value of its skin. Today in New Zealand opossums number millions. They raid orchards and suburban gardens, and interfere with power lines. All these animals feed on the leaves and young bark of trees,

The Dragon's Mouth geyser, Wairakei Valley. Pictured here is the world-famous Maori guide Rangi (Rangitiaria Dennan), who died in 1970. During her forty-three years as a guide, Rangi escorted many distinguished people, including Queen Elizabeth II and Prince Philip, on visits to the thermal regions.

n old-time kauri mdigger in Northnd. Over his shoulder n be seen a "gum ear", a long steel d attached to a spade ndle. The tool was eful in swamps for cating the pieces of m. An axe and spade re also essential ms of equipment.

Fertilising pastures by plane. New Zealand led the world in the development of aerial farming, much of which is now done by helicopter.

In a New Zealand dairy factory. Each of these giant churns can make more than two tons of butter at a time.

which subsequently die and thus expose the land to wastage.

Rabbits infest both crops and pastures, nibbling the grass right down to ground level, and burrowing among the roots so that the grass dies. The soil then blows away, or is washed out by rain, leaving stony desert areas where no sheep or cows can graze. The rabbits then fan out, widening the area of their destruction. As the result of their spread, in the 1870s the sheep population of one Otago station dropped from 120,000 to 45,000, while another in Southland fell from 50,000 to 20,000. By 1887 about a million and a half acres had been abandoned in these two provinces alone.

Both rabbits and opossums have proved amazingly persistent, and their drag on the national economy has been enormous; so the more that are shot, trapped, gassed or poisoned in New Zealand today the better — a far cry from the good old English custom of hanging or otherwise discouraging "moonlighters" who knocked off the occasional bunny to keep themselves and their families fed.

From the sportsman's viewpoint, the shooting of rabbits and hares still provides good and inexpensive sport in many New Zealand districts, besides receiving the blessing of both Government and landowner — though no rabbit may be bought in a New Zealand shop, no skins or carcasses can be exported, and even the children are prevented by law from keeping rabbits for pets. And since the red deer and the opossum, also, obstinately refuse to be eradicated, despite all the measures taken against them, it is clear that New Zealand will continue to be a hunter's paradise as well as an angler's for many years to come.

CHAPTER NINE

The Thermal Regions

Water h. and c.

New Zealand is unique in the number, variety and extent of her natural hot waters, which manifest themselves in countless hot springs and geysers, often associated with fumaroles and boiling mudpools. The most spectacular are at Rotorua, Wairakei and Orakeikorako, all fairly close together and within a few hours' drive from Auckland City.

At those places one may see examples of nature at her weirdest and most fantastic. Columns of steam and scalding water shoot skyward. Wide areas of boiling mud bubble and splutter like porridge in some giant cauldron. Whole lakes of boiling and near-boiling water may be seen at several places.

Hot pools lie side by side with cold ones, while some are hot in one part and cold in another. There, too, are broad translucent lakes, jade-green or azure-blue; gleaming terraces of silica — red, pink, yellow, or alabaster-white. Not far away is the vast expanse of Lake Taupo, twenty-five miles long, seventeen miles wide, overtopped by the three giant volcanoes Ruapehu, Ngauruhoe and Tongariro.

Hot Springs

Outside this main area are hundreds, probably thousands, of hot mineral springs and thermal muds. These occur at many places in the northern half of the North Island, from the central area south of Lake Taupo to the North Cape — a distance of over 300 miles. Near Whitianga, on the East Coast, hot springs bubble up from the seabed. In the South Island hot water issues from the ground at Hanmer, Maruia, and in some of the valleys of the Southern Alps.

Many of these springs have medicinal properties, and at some places, such as Rotorua, Hanmer, Te Aroha and Ngawha (in the far north) bath-houses have been built where people suffering from certain ailments may go to take the waters.

"The Rotorua waters are of two main kinds," wrote Dr J. D. C. Duncan, formerly balnaeologist to the New Zealand Government, "the 'Rachel' type, which is alkaline and sulphuretted, emollient to the skin and sedative in reaction; and the 'Priest' or free-acid type, which, due to the presence of free sulphuric acid, is mainly stimulating and tonic in reaction. There is also a valuable siliceous mud, similar to that found at Piest'any in Czechoslovakia.

"The Priest waters are used in the treatment of arthritis, fibrositis (the so-called rheumatic affections) and nervous debility. The Rachel and mud baths are effective in cases of fibrositis where the condition requires a softening effect, and for chronic skin diseases. In the types of affliction where pain is manifest, these baths have soothing and sedative qualities. They also reduce the swelling in affected joints and tissues. Many of the waters are radioactive, which may account for their therapeutic qualities; others derive their marked stimulative properties from an abundance of free carbonic acid gas." (New Zealand Official Year Book).

Very popular with the fit and well are the public mineral baths at Rotorua, focal point of the North Island tourist industry. Here at the famous Blue Baths the water is naturally heated; the pools are open to the air, and the water is therefore warm rather than hot. The Blue Baths building contains two pools, one for general use measuring a hundred feet by forty feet, and a smaller one specially for children. Diving platforms, underwater lighting, a cafeteria, filtration plants, and other amenities add to the attraction of these Baths, which are set in well-kept public gardens.

Medical treatment for the afflicted, once available in adjacent buildings, is now given at the Queen Elizabeth Hospital, where thermal pools, massage rooms and hydrotherapeutic equipment are provided.

Geysers and Fumaroles

In New Zealand, mineral springs are often associated with some form of volcanic activity. Of this the fumarole — an emission of steam, gas, or smoke from the earth's hot interior — is the prototype. Its variants are the blowhole, sending out dry steam at high pressure, and the geyser — all of which occur in variety in the main thermal areas at Rotorua, Wairakei, and Orakeikorako.

Geysers are perhaps the most fascinating features, and of these the now quiescent Waimangu was once the grandest of them all. From a mouth fifty yards across, it would periodically belch great rocks, and a column of steam and boiling water which sometimes shot as high as 1,500 feet in the air. Waimangu began suddenly in 1901, continued with daily displays for the next three years, then became intermittent. This geyser is now considered extinct, but its crater still holds the largest lake of boiling water in the world.

The New Zealand thermal regions are littered with the skeletons of extinct geysers, with their characteristic silica cones of varying height. There are, however, many beautiful and spectacular ones still active, as for example the lively Pohutu, at Whakarewarewa; the Lady Knox Geyser at Waiotapu, which plays every morning at 10 o'clock; the Eagle's Nest at Wairakei, with its triple jets, two of which play in unison and the other alone; and the Prince of Wales Feathers, which sends up a double or triple plume of boiling water as a prelude to Pohutu's scalding fury and clouds of steam.

Most geysers can be primed and made to play when specially required, but artificial stimulants are not now permitted except in the case of the Lady Knox Geyser. The addition of soap to the vent lightens the weight of the cooler top layer of water which the geyser has to eject before it really gets going. Somnolent blowholes and fumaroles can similarly be coaxed into action by holding a piece of burning rag or paper over the mouth.

Mineral deposits on surrounding sticks, rocks, logs, etc., often give fantastic shapes to the mouths of geysers. Notable examples are the Crow's Nest, the Eagle's Nest, and Dragon's Mouth, all spectacularly active. Others, such as the Papakura, the Dreadnought and the Cascade, are distinguished by the beauty of their mineral deposits, some of which form terraces, glowing with rich and iridescent colour.

The Pink and White Terraces

Finest of all were the magnificent Pink and White Terraces mentioned earlier, and called the "Eighth Wonder of the World" before their destruction in 1886 by the eruption of Mount Tarawera. These formations, several hundred yards wide at their base, have been described as "glittering crystal stairways, clear and stainless like ice, each spreading out like an open fan". The terraces covered more than seven acres, the steps varying in height from a few inches to twelve feet — in the most delicate shades of pink, white and turquoise. Their formation was the work of a geyser above, which for centuries had played on the mountain slope, first creating rippling falls, which in time grew into terraces. Today no one can say with certainty exactly where they lie buried.

At Orakeikorako the largest silica terraces in the world have been built up by the overflowing waters of hot pools and geysers, and they can be seen in the course of a conducted tour.

While it is clearly impossible to describe here all the various wonders of the New Zealand thermal regions — Aladdin's Cave at Orakeikorako; the Fairy, Rainbow and Paradise Valley Springs teeming with tame trout; the Twin Geysers, the Artist's Palette, the Dancing Rock, and the Paddlewheel — mention must be made of the famous Champagne Pool, or Cauldron, at Wairakei. This constantly seethes and roars in an unrivalled display of untamed natural energy — a witches' brew of gigantic size, sending up great clouds of steam and intermittent jets of scalding water. It has been estimated that to keep this Devil's Hot-pot going by artificial means would require 70,000 kilowatts of electricity.

Using Thermal Resources

For centuries, Maoris living in the thermal regions used the natural hot water there for cooking, washing clothes, and bathing. Many Europeans in that region have small wells from which they pipe hot water and sometimes steam, to heat their homes, schools, hotels. Some nurserymen heat glasshouses by similar means, while natural hot water is also used commercially by a few New Zealand industries.

Early in the 1950s, when power shortages were plaguing the country, New Zealand began investigating the possibility of harnessing her vast reserves of underground steam to generate electricity, as was being done at Lardarello, near Florence in Italy. Test bores were sunk in an effort to locate steam at pressures high enough to drive turbines.

These early probings obtained pressures of up to ninety pounds per square inch at depths ranging from 600 to 900 feet. One man-made geyser shot a column of steam 200 feet into the air when a drill-tip pierced the overlying strata. New Zealand scientists were sent to Italy to study the methods employed there, and to discuss problems which they might encounter . . . such as the corrosive action of the mineral-charged steam and the danger of explosions.

But drilling conditions at Lardarello are very different from those in New Zealand, where greater depths have to be penetrated and where the drills must punch through hot earth and rock. The problems thus encountered were quite without precedent. So New Zealand engineers had to work out their own techniques, and devise their own equipment — among them a means of deadening the ear-splitting roar usually emitted by active steam bores.

The result was that on 17 November 1958 the then Minister of Electricity (appropriately named Watt), opened at Wairakei New Zealand's first geothermal power station — the second in the world. Its output was then a modest 1700 kilowatts, but substantial development has followed, and Wairakei now contributes more than 150,000 kilowatts annually to the national grid.

To obtain the steam, bores of four, six and eight-inch diameter are drilled to depths of from 570 to 4,000 feet, and piped into generating plants. So far, thirteen of these plants have been built, the last in 1963. Recent test boring has located other promising reservoirs of underground steam, so the further development of this unusual source of power can be expected.

CHAPTER TEN

King Of The Forest

THE NEW ZEALAND KAURI ranks among the world's most impressive forest trees. Some still standing were alive when Alfred burned the cakes. Many reached prodigious size — one which grew at Mercury Bay was estimated to be twenty-four feet through, 150 feet high, and eighty feet from the ground to the lowest branch. From single trunks the Maoris fashioned mighty canoes, eighty feet long without break or join.

Showpiece today is "Tane Mahuta" (God of the Forest) which grows at Waipoua, in the far north. It has an overall height of 170 feet, a girth of forty-five feet six inches, and not one branch for the first forty-eight feet. Its age is estimated at over 1,200 years. Nearby in the same forest stands "Te Matua Ngahere" (Father of the Forest) which has a girth of fifty-three feet and contains 78,000 feet of millable timber — enough to build seven or eight wooden houses.

Before the white man came, majestic stands of kauri flourished throughout the northern half of the North Island, covering millions of acres. Today less than 26,000 acres remain, the largest area being the Waipoua Forest near Dargaville. Nursery work is proceeding there, and elsewhere, in an effort to regenerate the kauri forests; but since the trees take some 200 years to reach millable size, this project is essentially long-term.

Nevertheless there are still many places in the North Island where kauris may be seen growing singly or in clumps as part of the general forest scene, for example in the Waitakere Ranges, near Auckland and reached from that city in the course of a popular scenic drive. Small but impressive specimens grow in private and public gardens at New Plymouth, well south of the kauri's present normal home — though pollen found in South Island swamps indicates the kauri's presence there within quite recent geological times. It is thought that climatic changes have driven this tree northwards.

The Coromandel Peninsula, east of Auckland, is another region where the kauri still abounds, especially in the 160,000-acre forest park set aside by the government in 1970 to provide a "breathing space" for the rapidly expanding populations of Auckland and the Waikato. This area contains many kauris of great age and size, the remains of olden-day timber workings, kauri timber dams, and so on.

Because they were strong and resilient, and grew free from knots for scores of feet, kauri trunks made ideal spars and masts for sailing ships, including those of the Royal Navy, whose hulls of course were "heart of oak". But despite the abundance of this new source of timber, and its obvious suitability for many purposes, the kauri's commercial value seems to have escaped the notice of the earliest white explorers. The Frenchman, Marion du Fresne, however, leading his tragic expedition of 1772, first exploited this vast treasure awaiting discovery. As a result of storms while rounding North Cape, one of his ships had a damaged foremast which needed replacing. Du Fresne anchored in the Bay of Islands, established a shore station there, and soon found, at some distance inland, just what he wanted.

A fine kauri was felled and trimmed. The Maori owners were paid; and du Fresne then proceeded to astonish the natives by using a block and tackle to help get the trunk across miles of hilly country to the sea. Soon, however, trouble broke out, possibly through some infringement of the Maoris' tapu, and a number of Frenchmen, including du Fresne, were killed. His second in command, Crozet, bombarded the Maori settlement, causing heavy casualties, and then put to sea. Before long a flourishing export trade in kauri trunks sprang up, chief takers being the Royal Navy, Australian shipbuilders, and the East India Company.

Sawmilling, from its crude beginnings in the very early days, flourished with the systematic settlement of the country following the Waitangi Treaty of 1840. Timber was needed for the homes and furniture of the settlers, and for shops, schools, churches, and office buildings in the towns. Kauri proved ideal for all these. It was also used as shingles for roofs, even as footpaths in some places.

In those profligate days only heart timber went into such buildings, many of which still stand, as solid as the day they were built. An outstanding example is Wellington's huge block of Government offices, four storeys high and covering nearly two acres. This stands on Lambton Quay, close to the main railway station and directly opposite Parliament House. It is claimed to be the largest wooden building in the Southern Hemisphere.

Bullock teams, bush tramways, rafting and flooding by means of dams, the ruins of which can still be seen in some places, all contributed to the destruction of the kauri, as did the settler's axe and firestick. So today there is little of this timber available for milling. Its use is limited mainly to boatbuilding, and for finishing purposes.

Kauri Gum

When a kauri tree is damaged it "bleeds", exuding a sticky gum or resin which soon hardens, collecting in amberlike masses in the forks of the branches or around the roots. After the tree has fallen and rotted away, the gum remains in the ground; and over the centuries huge quantities accumulated in northern swamps and peatlands, the sites of long-vanished forests.

Kauri gum has proved useful in the manufacture of linoleum, paints, shellac and varnishes. It is also used to make gasket cement, and as bonding in dentistry, and the Germans have used it in making explosives. It is not surprising, therefore, that in the nineteenth century a unique industry, gum-digging, sprang up in New Zealand; in 1885 some 2,000 diggers were at work, mostly north of Auckland.

Today that industry is virtually defunct, though small quantities of the gum are still exported to England where it is sold by auction and re-exported to a number of countries. New Zealand farmers in the far north sometimes turn up kauri gum when digging or ploughing; and, when good prices are offering, they collect it for sale to merchants in Auckland.

The early diggers lived mostly in tents or shanties, often crudely made from sacking and saplings. Very few had wives wiht them, so they cooked their own rough tucker by primitive methods, living altogether a very hard life; so hard, in fact, that magistrates would order errant youths to spend some months at work on the gumfields. Many of the early diggers were hardy Yugoslavs who had come to avoid conscription into the Austrian army, and who sometimes returned, comparatively wealthy, to their own country when they were too old for military service under a foreign yoke.

There were two main methods of recovering kauri gum. One was by climbing the trees and hacking it out of the branch-forks. Because these were so far above the ground the diggers developed a special tree-climbing technique using spiked boots and small hand-picks — much as a mountaineer scales an ice face. A bag or pikau slung across the shoulders served to hold the gum.

The more general method was to probe the ground with spears up to fifteen feet long. Then the diggers used light, razor-sharp spades to unearth their find. At first the larger lumps, ranging in size from a fist to a football, were preferred; though the smaller pieces, called chips, also had their value.

Some of the oldtime diggers still survive in New Zealand, where they follow a variety of occupations; and one, Peter Vezich, recently gave the following graphic account to the writer Wayne Crawford for the *Auckland Star:*

I've dug down as far as twelve feet for gum. But it was so plentiful once it was nothing to dig as much as a full sack a day. You had to work for it though. Water would seep into the hole. You'd pull out a shovel of soil and then three or four buckets of water.

Out you'd come, covered with mud. Then on your back with the sack of gum and three-quarters of a mile back to camp.

I was sixteen when I started and it was hard work. I'd stagger and puff — but I couldn't put the sack down or I'd never get it onto my back again. When I did put it down at the camp I'd collapse.

But the digger's work day did not end then. He still had to spend long hours in the evening preparing the gum for market. For, after lying for centuries in the ground, it was usually mud-caked or impregnated. And few buyers would take the product unless it had been scraped — a long and tedious process.

Many diggers went further, and polished choice pieces (some lumps weighed up to thirty pounds) shaping them into hearts, crosses, spheres, and so on, for sale as souvenirs. The gum was even spun (it melted at around 150 degrees Celsius) and braided, then looking much like fine blonde hair. Such articles sold readily, and at one time New Zealanders up and down the country felt that their homes were hardly complete without their dozen or so kauri gum ornaments, proudly displayed in a glass-fronted cabinet, or laid out on mantelpiece and sideboard. Larger collections ran to hundreds, but few now remain except in museums.

At the turn of the century kauri gum fetched about $120 a ton; twenty years later the export price had risen to an average of $170, only to drop again in the depression of the thirties to about $50. In 1962 a shipment of one ton brought more than $600; but the quantity being sold has now diminished greatly, and nobody believes that this trade will ever recover. Stacked against that possibility are the dearth of easily recoverable gum, the competition of modern synthetics, and the spread of farming over the million or so acres of former swamp and wasteland where the diggers once followed their calling.

Although the old time Maori did not dig for kauri gum, he found several uses for the quantities he picked up on the surface. Fresh pieces were chewed, sometimes after being reduced to a more or less plastic state by heating. Kauri gum burns readily, and so it made excellent kindling, also torches; but its use as a fuel was limited because of excess smoke, and the comparative scarcity of supplies. Manuka scrub was much more readily available, and generally superior for firing. Powdered gum was sometimes mixed with the soot from burnt kahikatea (white pine) to make the pigment used in tattooing.

CHAPTER ELEVEN

Plant Rarities

BECAUSE OF ITS great number of endemic species the flora of New Zealand is remarkable. Such species number nearly 400, and they include more than 100 trees, sixty shrubs, forty-odd herbaceous plants, and some two dozen which are grasslike. Seventy-five per cent of New Zealand's indigenous flowering plants are not found anywhere else.

Though growing in a temperature zone, true New Zealand forests (known locally as "bush") are rain forests of either sub-tropical or sub-antarctic type. Most of the trees are evergreen, and the growth is luxuriant, with an exuberance of ferns and tree ferns, dense undergrowth, and an abundance of thick woody vines or lianes.

There is even a native palm, the nikau, which bears a rich crop of edible berries. This is the only true palm growing so far south of the equator, and its fronds were used for roofing by the Maori and by the very early white settlers. Equally remarkable is the so-called cabbage tree (called ti by the Maori) which is actually a giant lily — the tallest in the world. It grows to heights of up to forty feet.

Newcomers are often puzzled about the name of this tree, which some expect to find bearing cabbages. The name derives from its bushy crowns or leaf-masses, which grow at considerable heights from the ground and parts of which were cooked and eaten as a vegetable by early settlers. The Maoris, too, obtained food from this tree, but they preferred the long tap root, like a giant carrot two or three feet long, which provided them with one of their few sweet dishes.

These roots — actually underground extensions of the trunk — were dug out with sticks or hands and then steamed in the Maoris' large earth ovens called *hangi* or *umu*. When cool, the fibrous material of the root, now coated with a semicrystalline natural sugar, was dipped in water and chewed. Another method was to pound the cooked root in water to extract the sweet substance, which was said to resemble honey. Pounded fern-root, well cooked, was sometimes soaked in it to make a sweet or "pudding".

Leaves from the cabbage trees were sometimes used, along with the native flax, for plaiting canoe sails. Where flax was unobtainable, cabbage leaves also served for the making of kits (i.e. carrying baskets) and heavy waterproof cloaks. Early white settlers used the tall cylindrical boles — which have pithy centres, easily hollowed out — as chimneys for their huts.

Plant with a Past

Few plants have such a romantic history, or have been so closely woven into the life of a people, as the so-called New Zealand flax or *phormium* — not a true flax belonging to the genus linum or linseed, but a member of the agave family.

The Maoris recognised over sixty varieties of this plant, and they used the tough sword-shaped leaves of the harakeke, as they call it, in a number of ways. Thin strips, highly durable and virtually unbreakable, were excellent for tying and lacing; and they are still used for this purpose by both Maori and pakeha.

Broader strips were plaited to make belts and head-bands; baskets; food containers; canoe sails; floor matting, and platters called *kono* — each used only once — for meal times. Specially tough kinds went into the construction of shields or arm-bucklers. Vast quantities of the leaf were scraped and treated to obtain the tough fibre used by the Maori for his cordage and his clothing. In the weaving and dyeing of this fibre, as in its preparation for manufacture, his womenfolk gained a high expertise.

The value of the flax plant, especially for ropemaking, soon became known to the outside world, and a brisk trade sprang up long before the days of European settlement. The Maoris proved willing to sell, for they received in return not only the usual run of trade goods — nails, axes, blankets, shoddy clothing, rum and tobacco — but also a line they prized above all — muskets and ammunition for their tribal vendettas.

So, from 1810 on, small ships from Sydney and Hobart came

across the Tasman in quest of cargoes; and soon relays of Maoris were lugging heavy loads from far inland, or paddling them by river and sea to points on the coast where ships might call. Then, as the increased use of muskets rendered their hilltop forts untenable, and the need for counter-armaments grew, more and more Maoris went to live in the swampy, low-lying areas where flax grew, and fewer devoted themselves to food-growing.

The traders drove hard bargains, exchanging one musket, worth about a dollar, for every half-ton of flax fibre, laboriously cut and dressed with primitive tools, and representing a load which perhaps twenty women had carried on their backs for scores of miles along rough bush tracks.

While the export of flax fibre has now virtually ceased, much research has been done with this plant, and it is grown commercially in several places, notably around Foxton where large areas are cultivated. Flaxmills there make woolpacks, floor coverings, underfelt, and upholstery padding. Sometimes rope-makers mix flax fibre with sisal to make binder-twine, rope and other forms of cordage.

Nowadays flax bushes, which have rigid, swordlike leaves two inches to five inches wide and three feet to nine feet long, growing in fans, are becoming increasingly popular as garden plants. They bear large panicles of attractive red or yellow flowers on long woody stalks which sometimes reach a height of fifteen feet. These stalks when dry are light enough to float on water, so the Maoris often bound them in bundles to make rafts, called *moki*, or *mokihi*.

The Christmas Tree

A favourite with most New Zealanders, the pohutukawa is called the Christmas tree because in December it is ablaze with vivid crimson blossoms, dripping nectar.

The Maori name meaning, "splashed with spray", refers to its liking for growing on seacliffs and close to beaches. And many New Zealand coastal areas, including some of the larger towns, are strikingly ornamented by magnificent specimens. Auckland City, for example, has hundreds of them along its celebrated Tamaki Drive, and on its sea-cliffs.

One, still growing at Cape Reinga, marks the departure point, according to ancient Maori belief, of the souls of the dead when they set out for spirit-land. To the roots of another, at Kawhia, was tied the famous Tainui canoe which, around 1350 AD was one of a legendary Great Fleet bringing Maori migrants to this country.

Woman in the Moon

Yet another pohutukawa, according to Maori legend, once grew at Oma, near Leigh, some fifty-five miles north of Auckland, and now lives on the moon! An old *wahine* (Maori woman) then living at Oma scrambled one night, by the light of the full moon, down a steep cliff-track to fill a calabash of water at a spring. The moon went behind a cloud, and in the darkness the old woman tripped on the root of a pohutukawa.

Angrily she cursed the moon, which, likewise angered, then swooped down and seized her. She clung to the root, but without avail. She was carried, tree and all, up into the skies; and both can be seen there to this day, pohutukawa tree and woman.

Forest Oddities

The world's smallest conifer — *Dacridium laxifolium* — or pygmy pine, which bears fruit when only two or three inches high, is indigenous to New Zealand. At its maximum height, two or three feet, the stems are so weak and spindly that they can scarcely support the plant.

Also native to New Zealand (though it occurs, too, in the Norfolk, Tonga, and Fiji Islands) is the world's largest member of the violet family, the mahoe. Growing to heights of up to thirty feet, this tree bears on its thick branches masses of greenish-yellow flowers much smaller than the ordinary violet. Its common name, whitey-wood, derives from the appearance of the trunk, which is often covered with a white fungoid growth. The Maoris used the mahoe for making fire by friction.

Another tree, the brilliant-blossomed rata, is a notorious strangler. It begins life usually from a seed blown into the fork of some other tree. There it sprouts, and sends down "air roots" to form perpendicular columns which reach the ground. These columns then develop laterals which encircle the host tree and crush it in a deadly embrace. Often the rata's perpendicular pillars touch and grow together, forming a thick-walled tube. When in bloom the red rata flowers, which are not unlike those of the pohutukawa, throw a brilliant splash of colour across the green of the New Zealand forest.

The kotukutuku, or New Zealand fuchsia, is remarkable for having bright blue pollen. In the Auckland area this tree is deciduous; nearer Wellington it is evergreen. All four local types (*F. excorticata*, *F. colensoi*, *F. prucumbens* and *F. perscandens*) grow three distinct flower forms in each species.

Easily the world's rarest plant is the *tecomanthe speciosa*, of which only one exists in the wild state. A member of the bignonia family, this solitary plant grows on Great Island, one of the Three Kings group which lie north of Cape Reinga. In 1951, Professor G. T. S. Baylis brought back some material from this plant, and from it Mr J. A. Hunter of the New Zealand Department of Scientific and Industrial Research induced cuttings to grow at the Department's Plant Research Station in Auckland.

In 1956, seed-pods developed, the first ever seen by Europeans, and from these and other cuttings further propagation has been carried out. Large *T. speciosa* vines now grow in the Temperate House at Kew Gardens, England and in the Royal Horticultural Society's houses at Wisley.

Vegetable Sheep

Plants that grow "wool" and are often mistaken for sheep grow among the sub-alpine riverbeds of New Zealand's South Island. Known locally as "vegetable sheep", these plants are of the "patch" or "cushion" type, and are a species of Raoulia. Their tiny, close-packed leaves grow a covering of fine threads like silk or wool. White in summer and autumn, they assume a handsome chocolate colour for the remainder of the year.

Besides vegetable sheep, New Zealand also has vegetable caterpillars, creatures found also in Australia, and which flout the laws of nature by being both animal and vegetable.

They begin life as caterpillars of the Porina moth, crawling on a leaf-strewn forest floor. Onto the back of the caterpillar falls a spore from a fungus called *cordyceps robertsii*. The spore

Portrait of the Maori warrior Patuone, by Gottfried Lindauer
(1839–1926)

Maori treasure boxes (*Waka huia* or *papaou*) photographed on a cloak in the Dominion Museum, Wellington.
The interior of Te Hau Ki Turanga, a meeting house built many years ago and now reassembled in the Dominion Museum, Wellington.

Symbol of New Zealand, the kiwi, a nocturnal flightless bird.

A giant kauri tree, king of the forest.

A dairy herd in Taranaki, North Island, with Mt Egmont in the background.

Sheep of the high country, South Island (Glentanner sheep station).

The smoking volcano Mt Ngauruhoe, North Island.

Mitre Peak reflected in Milford Sound, South Island.

promptly germinates and pierces the caterpillar's skin. The grub then burrows into the ground with the idea of becoming a chrysalis; but before it can do so the fungus, growing rapidly, invades every part, right to the tiny claws, and fills it with a woody mass of vegetable matter.

After a time a clublike shoot grows from the head, and eventually protrudes about two inches above ground. On this develop the spores or "seeds". Millions are dispersed; but the life-cycle can resume only when one chances to fall on the back of a Porina caterpillar. Specimens have been found up to three and a half inches long, with the total length of the sprouted shoot measuring over five inches.

The Kowhai

No account of New Zealand's flora would be complete without some mention of the kowhai, one variety of which has been represented pictorially on the current two-cent piece, on the oldtime penny, and on the threepenny stamp of the pre-decimal era. These are depictions of the golden kowhai, a magnificent blossom specially adapted to pollination by birds.

The flowering of the golden kowhai is a gay harbinger of spring, especially in the Auckland province, where it grows profusely on trees often over twenty feet high; and the Maoris used it to set the time for their potato-planting. The flowers sometimes mass on otherwise bare branches, with the curled-up leaf buds unfolding later. Other varieties bear leaves and blossoms simultaneously.

A distinctively different type of kowhai is the kaka beak, named because of the blossom's similarity in shape to the beak of the kaka — a native parrot. This blossom is usually deep red, sometimes white, in colour and it grows on a dark glossy green shrub. The kaka beak is used both in New Zealand and overseas as an ornamental shrub, and it makes a good pot plant. Scientific name is *Clianthus puniceous* meaning plant with a glorious blood-red flower.

CHAPTER TWELVE

Those Green Pastures

AUSTRALIA HAS BEEN CALLED "the sunburnt country". New Zealand by contrast is a land of green pastures; and no country on earth relies so heavily on grass for its national income. Nowhere are meadows greener, or a more pervading feature of the landscape; and nowhere does grass grow more quickly.

Yet all these emerald fields have been man-made, in little more than a century — along with the building of railways, roads, seaports, airfields, schools, houses, cities, and the development of secondary industries. Before that the country was mostly forestclad, with few natural grasslands. Only reeds, scrub and rough tussock grew on the treeless areas. Even the original grass-seed had to be imported, yet today large quantities of grass-seed, highgrade and government-tested, are sold abroad.

This conversion of the country from bush and swamp to grassland was no easy matter, for New Zealand soils are not naturally fertile, as many people believe. Most of them are deficient in phosphorus, and many lack lime and certain other plant foods. So, after being laid down, New Zealand pastures must be constantly treated with top dressings of phosphate and other fertilisers.

This was once a very laborious business, with the farmer carting or sledging the heavy manure, or taking it by packhorse to his hilly "outback" areas. There he humped great loads on his back, slowly spreading the stuff by hand. Topdressing in this way often took several months to complete.

Farming from the Air

Today many New Zealand farms are fertilised in just a few hours by the use of aircraft. Agricultural flying was pioneered in

New Zealand; and this country still leads in the use of planes and helicopters for such purposes as back country fencing, liming, seedsowing, deer culling, weed eradication, orchard spraying, and rabbit destruction. Yet, spectacular though this development has been, it is only one of a long series of measures which have established New Zealand as the world's leader in pasture management.

The result is that in a small mountainous country, those green pastures now support more than sixty million sheep; over three million high-grade dairy cattle; a large pig population, fed mostly on skim milk or whey; and four and a half million head of beef cattle. New Zealand now has, in fact, more than twenty-five times as many animals as people, a ratio probably the highest in the world. Her best dairy farms carry one cow to the acre, while the best sheep farms can support up to ten sheep to the acre throughout the year. These flocks and herds live the year round out of doors, i.e. on pasture, with supplementary feeding mainly of hay and silage made from the surplus pasture growth of spring and early summer. Virtually no grazing animals except horses are housed during winter.

New Zealand is now a leading cheese exporter, has long been the world's largest exporter of butter, and (in some years) of meat. She holds third place in the world as a producer of wool, and second place as an exporter. More crossbred apparel wool is exported from New Zealand than from any other country, and wool production per acre there is the highest in the world. Similar records can be claimed for the best New Zealand dairylands, where the annual production of butterfat per acre reaches 350 to 400 pounds, while the national average yield per cow is about 300 pounds of butterfat a year.

These achievements have not come easily. They are the result of hard work, careful planning, and highly scientific methods of farming, processing, transport and marketing. They are a far cry from those not-too-distant early days when the dairyman's cows roamed in the bush at will, and were milked whenever they could be found; or when sheep carcasses were boiled down for tallow, that being their only commercial product. The story changed dramatically, of course, with the introduction of refrigerated transport in 1882. From then on, New Zealand no longer depended on Australia as a market for her butter and cheese; they could now be sent to Britain and Europe, where prices were higher, the demand greater. Meat, too, could now be exported; and so a great new era of trading and production began.

The first sheep to reach New Zealand were two Merinos brought by Captain Cook, but they soon died. The first flock, also Merino, imported from Australia, was established in 1834 on a small island near Wellington. Other Merino flocks followed; but these animals, of a species originally from Spain, while growing a very fine wool, are rather scraggy and carry little meat. English breeds did better among the logs and blackened stumps of New Zealand's early "bush-burn" country; but while those breeds produced good meat, their wool did not compare with that of the Merino.

A solution was found by mating the Merino with English strains such as the Romney, the Southdown and the Lincoln to produce a "crossbred" or dual purpose animal yielding well in both wool and meat. One outcome of this crossing was the evolution in New Zealand of an entirely new sheep breed — the Corriedale, which is now raised in Australia, China, Kenya, India, Argentina, Chile, Israel and Scotland.

Grazing the Skyline

Today Merino sheep are still grazed among the mountains of New Zealand's Southern Alps, at altitudes of up to 6,000 feet, where they have put their own unique crimp into the story of wool.

This high country is hard on both man and beast. The climate is rigorous, the terrain forbidding; yet the Merino and its crosses thrive on it. Their fodder consists mostly of the coarse native tussock, or snowgrass. In spring the sun melts the snow and uncovers pastures at the lower levels. The sheep feed on these and then as the season advances they follow the receding snowline to its mid-summer limits. In autumn they start moving down again to escape the devastation of heavy snow and blizzards.

CHAPTER THIRTEEN

Forests Made By Man

TIMBER HAS ALWAYS played an important part in New Zealand's national life. Over a long period wood was the principal material used for fuel, fencing and building; and at first it was virtually the only satisfactory substance available for such purposes. In the early 1850s timber was New Zealand's chief export. Today forest products — sawn timber, logs, wood pulp, newsprint, cardboard and so on — rank fourth on the country's list of exports, their value exceeded only by those of wool, meat and dairy products.

For many years New Zealand bushmen felled and milled only the native trees, though as early as 1874 a Forests Act provided that Crown land could be devoted to the development of State forests. Nevertheless, afforestation, confined at first to the planting of quick-growing exotic trees, began very slowly in New Zealand, and by 1913 the country's total acreage, including shelterbelts planted by farmers, trees grown by local bodies for beautification, or to check erosion, amounted to only 65,000 acres. Fifty years later, this total exceeded a million acres, and it is still increasing.

Between 1923 and 1936 the Government planted 370,000 acres, nearly all of it radiata pine, introduced from California, while in the same period commercial companies planted some 290,000 acres of radiata. This activity centred on three main areas: the North Auckland scrublands which formerly yielded kauri gum; similar type country in the Nelson province; and the vast volcanic plateau which extends northward and eastward from Lake Taupo in the North Island. Here the Government established its Kaingaroa State Forest, which now covers more than 300,000 acres and is claimed to be the world's largest man-made forest.

Much of the planting on the Kaingaroa Plain was done as "relief work" during the depression of the 1930s; and although more than half the trees are radiata pine, plantations of other species such as the Ponderosa pine, the Corsican pine, and the Douglas fir (Oregon pine) were also established and are now being harvested. All these reach millable size more quickly in New Zealand than in any other country.

The soil in this area derives mostly from pumice ejected many centuries ago by volcanoes of the Thermal Region, and those people who tried to farm the land found that their stock contracted a mysterious wasting disease called "bush-sickness" — similar to that known in other countries as "pine" or "vinquish". The trouble has since been found to be a deficiency of trace elements in the soil, notably cobalt. Since the Second World War land development has been carried out on a very large scale and areas opened up for farming. Meanwhile this "worthless" area proved ideal for forestry and its contingent industries. The large modern mills that have been built, notably at Tokoroa, Kinleith, Pinedale, Waipa and Kawerau, are equipped with the latest in modern machinery and serviced by experts. Large modern towns have grown up near some of the mills to supply housing and other needs.

Development in the Kaingaroa State Forest follows a Working Plan — a formal legal document in which are set down full and detailed prescriptions for the Forest's long-term management. The port of Tauranga, fifty-four miles north of Rotorua, has been enlarged to handle the increasing volume of products, many of them destined for overseas markets, that are now pouring in from the mills and forests.

Today New Zealand's resources of *Pinus radiata* provide more than half the sawn timber used locally, and could in fact supply all of it. The only uses for which this product is not suited are furniture-making and joinery.

Nevertheless, New Zealand builders, long accustomed to working with the durable "heart" woods yielded by their native trees — kauri, rimu, totara, and so on — did not take kindly to using the new exotic timbers, which are almost entirely sapwood. Nor did the building authorities readily sanction their use. And so there has developed in New Zealand a notable timber treatment and preservation industry, by far the world's largest on a per capita basis, and the world's most efficient for the benefit of the building industry and of the general public.

CHAPTER FOURTEEN

The New Zealand Gourmet

"TAKE ONE CUP OF WHITEBAIT, mix with batter, fry lightly in a hot pan, then serve as fast as it disappears." And that will be *very* fast if you follow this recipe for one of the world's most tasty dishes — whitebait fritters, a favourite at breakfast, lunch or teatime in New Zealand homes. But of course there are many different ways of cooking whitebait, with or without the use of batter.

"Teatime" in New Zealand is usually around five or six in the evening — North America's "suppertime". But the New Zealand meal taken then is often called "dinner", instead. The theory seems to be that if this is the main meal of the day, dinner is the proper term, and the midday meal is then "lunch". But if the lunchtime meal is the main one, it becomes dinner, and the later one is "tea".

To confuse the issue still further, your New Zealander will often take "afternoon tea", somewhere round 3 or 4 pm — a cup of tea or coffee and a snack. The cup of tea is made the true English way and unspoiled by teabags while coffee is especially popular if percolated from freshly-ground beans, though the "instant" kinds also are widely used.

Supper arrives between the main night meal and bedtime — generally about 9 or 10 o'clock, and is much the same as afternoon tea.

But to return to our whitebait. Fish known by that name are caught elsewhere, e.g. in Britain; but the New Zealand whitebait occurs only in this country, where it ranks as a national delicacy; and in Australia (where it rarely, if ever, appears as a comestible) and in South America.

Until lately this slender creature with its transparent body only an inch or two long, and its prominent dark eyes which stare up reproachfully when cooked, was something of a mystery. People knew that every year from July to November it swarmed up the creeks and rivers in dense shoals, to be caught in nets and eaten. But the whitebait's life history long remained a matter for uninformed speculation, and many a rash wager.

Scientists have now worked out the answer. The whitebait, known to them as *Galaxias attenuatus*, is spawned by a species of freshwater minnow commonly called the "yellow-belly", but known to the Maori as inanga. Adults of this fish, a species of native trout, grow to a length of five or six inches, are greenish-yellow in colour, and found in most New Zealand rivers and streams.

In autumn this minnow swims downstream to lay its eggs under the grass and weeds of tidal estuaries. This is done at springtide, in places which will not be submerged again until the next spring tide, two weeks later. By that time the spawn has been hatched and the larvae pass out into the sea.

It is still not certain whether the young fish return to the rivers in the first or the second spring after hatching, but it is thought that the spawn remain for about five months at sea, close to the coastline, where large quantities are inevitably eaten by other marine creatures — for the whitebait has no natural protection other than its transparency. The numbers originally hatched must be astronomical. Then the survivors congregate in dense shoals to swim back up the rivers, to start the life cycle all over again. Though still transparent at this stage, they soon become pigmented after entering fresh water.

Every year some four or five hundred tons of whitebait are captured, many finding their way to canneries which have been established near some of the larger rivers. The fish are caught in fine-mesh nets, but, in the interests of conservation, the Government limits not only the size of the nets, but also the proximity of one fisherman to the next, the duration of the fishing season, the devices which may be used to entice the whitebait into the nets, and so on.

With the clearing of riparian lands and estuaries the minnows are deprived of their natural spawning grounds, so that many streams which could be fished quite profitably a generation ago now yield scant harvests or none at all. Modern transport also is tending to "thin out" the whitebait, since more fishermen can now go by car to streams that once lay beyond their reach.

The harvest is a profitable one when the fish are running well, and some commercial fishermen either deep-freeze their catch or hire aircraft to get it fresh to the city markets. From there it is distributed throughout the country via the normal retail channels, and surpluses are frozen for sale in the off-season. Housewives find that this favoured food costs no more on a meal-for-meal basis than the usual run of available fish.

The Toheroa

Similarly esteemed as a delicacy is the toheroa, a large shell-fish of the clam family found only in New Zealand. But these fish too are becoming less easy to get; and the taking of toheroas, which are dug up from damp sand on a few North Island beaches and on some Southland beaches bordering Foveaux Strait, is now limited to a brief season each year — usually in the months of July and August.

The purpose of this restriction is to aid the regeneration of toheroa beds, which are subject to depletion through natural causes. When this becomes severe, the beds are closed to the public altogether, sometimes for several years on end.

A good average toheroa grows to about five inches long, three inches wide, and an inch and a half thick. Its age would be some twelve or thirteen years. On the shell it weighs about a pound. The meat is made into delicious soup, or it may be served as fritters equally appetising. But the flesh of the toheroa is naturally tough, and skill is needed to obtain the best results.

Since the "discovery" of toheroa soup by the Duke of Windsor (then Prince of Wales) while on a visit to New Zealand in 1920, this dish has become a favourite with epicures and bon viveurs in many countries. In 1935 two New Zealand canneries processed some 400,000 toheroas; but twenty years later only one factory was operating, and the total annual output had dropped to about one third the previous figure.

Toheroas feed on diatoms or plankton, a minute form of vegetable life which supplies the toheroa with chlorophyl. This gives the soup its characteristic green colour, and its high nutritive value. The toheroa gets its daily ration by sucking in seawater through a tiny tube, extracting the nutriment, then ejecting the remainder through a second tube. These tubes extend above the surface as the shellfish lies hidden some four to eight inches under the sand.

There it is safe from most natural enemies; and there at low tide it is eagerly sought, in the season, by hordes of people, men, women and children, Maori and pakeha. In the past, weapons of attack have included spades, shovels, and tyre levers. But some years back such implements were forbidden, and only wooden ones were permitted. Now they too are banned, and he who wants to take toheroas legally must dig for them with his hands. Even then there are limits on the catch; and at all toheroa beaches fisheries inspectors keep a sharp eye out for poachers.

On Northland's famous Ninety Mile Beach, the traditional home of the toheroa, fish have been seen at low tide to swim inshore with the bigger waves, nip off the toheroa's suckers and then dart out to sea again as the water recedes. But the biter may be bitten; and many an unwary snapper has been caught with his water down, doing a head-stand.

The Huhu

Anyone lost in the New Zealand bush could subsist for quite a time on the food it provides — as many a straying tramper, and servicemen on exercises, have had to do. One item of "tree food" freely available is the huhu, a juicy grub about three inches long and as thick as a man's forefinger, found in rotting logs. Actually the larva of a large beetle, the huhu is esteemed as food by Maoris, and by some Europeans who have acquired a taste for it.

At one public banquet in Wellington, attended by the Governor-General, this delicacy featured on the menu, and New Zealand's then Prime Minister ate a number of huhus. One may eat them fried in butter, when they are crunchy, like peanuts; or alive and gently wriggling.

The Paua

Living off the seashore is even easier in New Zealand than living off the land, for the coastline — an exceptionally long one, with innumerable inlets, bays, sounds, fiords and estuaries — is liberally endowed with a variety of edible shellfish. All these are tasty and nutritious, and, with a few exceptions such as the toheroa, the mussel, the scallop and the oyster, are free for the taking at any time. Yet, strangely enough, until quite recently many of these shellfish were largely neglected as a source of food by the European population, though not by the Maori, who traditionally ate large quantities.

One such shellfish is the paua, a univalve rather like an outsized limpet though more ear-shaped, found clinging to submerged coastal rocks, generally just beyond the low-tide level. With a flattened oval shell, and a row of holes along the back, the paua grows to a length of about six inches. Related species are the muttonfish of Australia and the abalone of North America, which rates as a delicacy and fetches high prices.

The paua has great powers of suction and its removal from a rock calls for skill and cunning rather than brute force. The shrewdest move is a quick thrust with a thin-bladed knife between rock and fish while the latter is quietly day-dreaming. The meat is prepared by discarding all the soft parts, also the long white ribbon-like structure which contains the creature's innumerable tiny teeth, and retaining only the tough foot and muscle. This has an unattractive black coating which may be removed by rubbing. The meat can either be minced and frittered, or tenderised by pounding, then rolled in flour, and grilled for no more than three minutes. Either way makes a delectable repast.

The Pipi

Several species of pipi, and their cousins the cockles, may be taken by the hundredweight from numerous New Zealand bays and estuaries, subject to certain conditions. Closely related to the clams of North America, Hawaii, and elsewhere, pipis can be baked, steamed or made into chowder. They are equally delicious when minced and served as fritters. Many people prefer to eat them like oysters — raw, and still alive.

Oysters

According to the writer Saki (H. H. Munro), "oysters are more beautiful than any religion. There's nothing in Christianity or Buddhism which matches the sympathetic unselfishness of an oyster."

New Zealand has its own distinctive species, one of which is harvested during a season limited by Government decree. For three months of the year fresh supplies come on the market in large quantities — but not large enough to satisfy public demand — from coastal beds in the Auckland province. These are rock oysters, under strict control by the Marine Department since 1908.

At the other extreme geographically are vast beds of the Stewart Island oyster dredged from the seabed in or near Foveaux Strait under freer conditions and for a longer season. In earlier days it was possible, in some places near the shore, to fill an eighteen-ton cutter in a couple of days by the simple process of stranding the boat on the beds at low tide, then scrambling over the side and cramming sacks or baskets. But that method, of course, soon cleaned out the more accessible spots.

The northern oysters are smaller and sweeter, but more difficult to take from the shell. Both species are delicious when eaten alive (and your true oyster-fancier must have them that way) or they may be served, as with oysters anywhere, in soups, stews, curries, patties, scalloped, and so forth.

Muttonbirds

The origin of this name, which was probably coined by early white settlers of New Zealand and Australia, is something of a mystery, since neither the taste of the flesh nor its appearance has much affinity with mutton. Perhaps in the struggling, meat-scarce early days this food was a mutton-substitute; or possibly the name derives from the woolly appearance of the chicks, whose plump downy bodies provide the comestible.

The birds themselves, which are about sixteen inches long, are well-known to science as species of petrels or shearwaters: the short-tailed shearwater which frequents the coastal waters of Tasmania and southern Australia; the grey-faced petrel found on islands off the Auckland coastline; and the sooty shearwater of the Foveaux Strait area which supplies the New Zealand market.

On islands in or near that Strait the New Zealand mutton-birders, restricted now to Maoris and their families, ply their unusual trade. In a brief season which opens at the beginning of April and continues through to mid-May they "knock off" the young birds just before they are able to fly, pluck the down which has a commercial value, and preserve the bodies which yield food and oil. About 250,000 chicks are taken in a year and distributed mainly to fish shops thoughout the country.

Eels Aplenty

Oddly enough pakeha New Zealanders are not, like their British cousins and many other Europeans (e.g. the Dutch), dedicated eel-eaters. For sure there are eels aplenty in most swamps and rivers. Country kids catch them for sport, but seldom take them home to be cooked. Eels are even "tamed", by some people with quaint ideas about pets, fed by hand, and, it is claimed, induced to wriggle right out of the water.

For centuries the Maori has feasted on eel, which he calls tuna, and it still one of his favourite foods. He caught this fish most often in a large elongated basket called a hinaki. This he set in running streams; or, in late autumn, at the outfalls from flooded swamps, when large numbers of eels were "on the run" — following the receding waters to return to the rivers — and as many as 700 eels have been taken this way at one haul.

Before setting his hinaki the fisherman builds a v-shaped weir extending usually from bank to bank and converging to a narrow opening where the trap is placed. To make the weir he first drives stakes of manuka (a native shrub) or other light timber into the ground. The fence or palisade thus erected is then lined with bundles of fern and manuka branches.

The catch, ranging up to about thirty inches in length, is tipped out on to clear ground where the squirming creatures are despatched by whacking each one on the tail with a heavy stick. Then follows cleaning, which might take a whole day if the haul is a large one. To remove their coating of slime, the eels are immersed in hot water and then rubbed down with stiff fern-tops.

For the cooking a huge fire is made, usually of manuka, the twiggy, tiny-leaved branches of which, when dry, become like tinder and burn with a fragrant smoke. The burnt sticks form glowing coals, holding their heat and their glow for hours. Onto these hot embers the food is placed.

An account of one such "eel-bake" was told by Harry Taituha with characteristic Maori charm and humour for the *New Zealand Weekly News:*

We staked each eel with a skewer cut out of fern-stalks and drove it through from head to tail. This would make for easier handling and turning on the fire. It would also stop the eel breaking when cooked.

We cooked the eels in lots of 100 at a time. At least the old man did; Ngeru and I were too busy eating. The old man had his eels lined up against a rack in front of the huge fire like a battalion of greasy soldiers.

The heat, the drips and the crackle of roasting tuna soon had the place smelling like a kitchen and it wasn't long before we had friends and relatives paying us that long-put-off visit. The old man made it an open house for everybody.

Not all eels are suitable for cooking in this manner. Swamp tunas such as we got out of the Kahahoroa swamp are the best because they live on mud and are fat, and the Maori likes it fat — especially the tail. This part of the tuna is always given to the women. That's Maori etiquette. The old man, himself a product of the old school, never touched an eel until everybody had had their fill.

We didn't gut them. The old man said there was no need to because they were clean, their food consisting chiefly of mud. River eels would have to be cleaned, said the old man. They weren't particular about what they ate. But swamp eels were different; they were clean mud eels.

Nevertheless, when it came to eating Ngeru and I steered clear of the funny parts and ate only the good. We ate and ate and went to sleep in the long grass.

Other ways of taking eels include spearing and "bobbing". The latter method consists of threading worms with flax or twine, tying the result into a "bob" or bundle, then dangling it in the water from a line on the end of a stick. Often the fish are enticed to the spot by throwing in rotten eggs, food scraps, or offal.

When an eel takes the bob the fisher flicks his line up and lands it, complete with fish, on the bank behind him. There the eel soon releases the bob which, by catching in his teeth, has caused his undoing. Hooks are sometimes used, but are less easy to detach.

Maoris sometimes grope for swamp eels with their hands, especially in summer when the water level is low. They know the likeliest places to probe, and also how to grasp the eel — by the head, so as not to lose a finger or two.

Smoked eel sells at a medium price in New Zealand shops, but the demand is comparatively light. Recently an export trade has developed, mainly to markets in Europe, where this fish fetches high prices.

Tropical Foods

When the Maoris first arrived from northern Polynesia they probably brought with them tropical plants such as the banana and the breadfruit, which do not normally survive in temperate zones. They had more luck with their taro and yams (though the taro is seldom grown in New Zealand now) and with kumara, which is cultivated in large quantities and highly esteemed by both Maori and pakeha.

In recent years a number of tropical and sub-tropical food-plants have become established, some with spectacular success. An outstanding example is the tamarillo, once called the tree-tomato, (*Cyphomandra betacea*), a native of South America. This fruit now grows prolifically, and is cultivated commercially in many northern New Zealand areas. It enjoys a ready sale on local markets, and a promising export trade is developing.

With a fruiting season which lasts from May to November, right through the southern winter, the tamarillo is a great stand-by for New Zealand housewives when other fruits and vegetables are scarce, and its uses are numerous.

The tamarillo may be prepared as follows for a tasty and nourishing breakfast dish, now a favourite in many New Zealand homes:

Soak about a dozen (each is about the size of a duck egg) in boiling water for half an hour, then peel and halve them. Two or three halves suffice for one serving. Place the halves in a saucepan of hot syrup (sugar and water) and simmer for five minutes. Serve either hot or cold. Prepared that way the tamarillo can also be used as a dessert, either by itself or with custard or ice-cream.

Two varieties are grown, one having an attractive shiny red skin, the other yellow. Both are rich in vitamin C. The red is more "tangy"; the yellow has a milder and sweeter flavour. Unaccustomed eaters often approach this food rather warily, despite its attractive appearance; but a taste for it is soon acquired.

The tamarillo grows on bushy trees from six to twelve feet high, so it is easily harvested. The fruit has a tough skin which protects it while on the way to market, so it needs no individual wrapping. Each tree — grown from either seed or cuttings — averages from forty to sixty pounds in a year, 400 bushels to the acre, for ten or twelve years. Crops can be harvested from eighteen months to two years after planting.

Kiwi Fruit

Once called the Chinese gooseberry, and now rechristened with dubious felicity, this fruit also is exported from New Zealand to a number of countries including Great Britain and the United States. A member of the Dilleniaceae family, the plant's native home is the Yangtse valley in China. Its fruit, about the size and shape of a blunt-ended hen egg, has a thin but tough brown skin, covered which soft bristles like those of the gooseberry. It has no connection whatever with the kiwi, which, as every schoolboy knows, does not lay fruit.

This product, while less adaptable then the tamarillo, has an exquisite flavour and is generally eaten raw by scooping out the soft flesh with a teaspoon. It gives a lift to a fruit salad and looks and tastes well on cream cakes and pavlovas.

A most valuable use is as a booster for the poorer cuts of meat. Thin slices are spread on the meat for ten minutes, no longer; enzymes in the fruit make the meat more tender, and

A giant crane lifts a thirty-ton load of logs from a railway truck at a New Zealand paper mill. Timber, paper and forest products are fourth on the list of New Zealand's exports.

Maori skindiver with a haul of paua. The fish is eaten, the shell made into jewellery.

improve its flavour. An over-long application spoils the meat's texture.

Etceteras

Other tropical or semi-tropical fruits which grow readily in New Zealand include the feijoa, the guava, and the delicious "black" passion-fruit, a *sine qua non* of any self-respecting New Zealand fruit salad. Passion-fruit grow prolifically on leafy vines, are spherical or ovoid, and have a tough dark-purple skin, filled with a sweet seedy pulp. They are often eaten in the same way as the kiwi fruit — by slicing in half and scooping out the pulp with a spoon. Jam is often made from passion-fruit, and the raw pulp is spread on pavlovas, which we shall discuss in a moment.

With such a variety of foodstuffs available to her at reasonable prices, the New Zealand housewife is blessed indeed. Usually she has her own kitchen garden, and often a few fruit trees. Meat, of course, is plentiful in a land which exports millions of tons of it; and most kinds — beef, mutton, lamb, veal, pork and bacon — are cheaper in New Zealand than in most other countries. So too are milk, butter and a wide variety of cheeses. Poultry, on the other hand, is more expensive than in, say, North America.

Many grape varieties grow well in New Zealand, where a flourishing wine industry has developed. A number of the local wines can compete in quality with imported kinds and, under a government "protectionist" policy, remain comparatively cheap in price. Brandy has been distilled experimentally under government supervision, with a view to commercial production in New Zealand.

Hearty Eaters

It is not surprising that a recent survey by the United Nations placed New Zealand well up on its list of the world's biggest eaters, with a daily calorie intake of 3,430, second only to Eire's 3,500. And while the following menu would not be typical of meals taken *en famille*, it could be matched, with the addition of soups and sweets, in a number of the best hotels. It is actually the fare provided by the New Zealand Wine and Food Society to entertain a distinguished French gourmet at a buffet dinner featuring New Zealand foods:

Smoked snapper roe on toast
Scallops in the shell turned in butter
Whitebait fritters
Smoked eel poached in local white wine and chicken stock
Venison casseroled in New Zealand red wine
Cold roast wild pork with apple sauce
Beetroot marinated in lemon juice and honey
Roast kumara wrapped in bacon
Tomatoes stuffed with mushrooms served on lettuce leaves
Fresh corn off the cob
Green asparagus with mayonnaise
New Zealand cheese board
Fresh fruit

But here is another sample of local eating as reported in a Press Association message headed ONE COARSE MEAL:

A slightly-built Maori walked into a Waitara restaurant looked at the menu and completely staggered the waitress by, announcing, "I'll have the lot."

The girl returned with an enormous silver tray laden with steak, bacon, oysters, sausages, omelette, fish and chips, and eighteen eggs.

The customer, watched by several amazed patrons and the entire restaurant staff, attacked the mountain of food and cut it right down to a few chips and three sausages before deciding he was comfortably full.

He completed the meal by drinking four bottles of soft drink, wrapped the remaining sausages and chips to take away, paid his four-dollar bill and left.

That Pavlova

So many visitors to the country comment ecstatically on this cake, and it is greeted with such surprised delight whenever New Zealand hostesses produce it overseas that it rates as a national delicacy and may well take its place on the New Zealand gourmet's coat-of-arms, with whipped cream rampant.

Baked in an ordinary sandwich tin, a successful pavlova consists of a crisp, pale-gold outer shell of meringue containing fluffy white marshmallow. It is turned out on to a plate, soft part uppermost, and spread thickly with whipped cream. On to that are placed fresh strawberries, raspberries, passionfruit pulp, or slices of Chinese gooseberry. One favourite recipe runs as follows:

Three egg whites; one teacup sugar; one teaspoon vinegar; one teaspoon vanilla essence; a pinch of salt.

Add salt to egg-whites and beat till very stiff. Add sugar, a tablespoonful at a time, beating well after each addition. Then beat in the vinegar and essence.

Line sandwich tin with butter papers (greasy side up) after they have been held under a cold tap then shaken to remove surplus water. This lining should extend about two inches above the rim of the tin, to allow for similar rise in the "cake". Fill lined tin with mixture. Bake for one hour at around 300 degrees.

If baking on a wet day, warm the sugar before using.

CHAPTER FIFTEEN

North Island Features

The Waitomo Caves

"For outstanding attractiveness and infinite charm New Zealand has no equal in any part of the world." So declared Lord Bledisloe, a former Governor-General; and he ascribed that charm mainly to the great variety of the New Zealand scenery. In many parts, at almost every turn of the road the traveller can find some fresh view, or some arresting natural masterpiece.

A number of these have already been described: the volcanoes, the thermal region, Lake Taupo, Kaingaroa State Forest — all in the North Island. In that Island, too, are the famous Waitomo Caves, about twelve miles from the inland town of Te Kuiti, and only six miles by good road from the main highway and the Main Trunk Railway linking Auckland with Wellington.

Three geat caves comprise the group, two of them — Aranui and Ruakuri — being typical limestone caverns with stalactites and stalagmites in an extraordinary range of forms and groupings. Near these, and only a few hundred yards from a fine modern tourist hotel, is the matchless Glow-worm Grotto, in the cave called Waitomo, where one can "leave the world of today and enter the world of a million yesterdays". All three caves may be explored during a morning or an afternoon, and guides from the hotel conduct all parties of visitors.

Waitomo Cave was first discovered in 1887 by a surveyor's assistant, Fred Mace. Accompanied by Tane Tinorau, a local Maori, Mace set out on a flimsy raft to explore the Waitomo River beyond the point where it disappears underground through a hole in the cliff. Today visitors enter at a different point — a crevice in the cliff which they can reach by a brief walk from the hotel along a pleasant bush track. Once inside they are impressed by the uncanny stillness of the air, and by the temperature, which remains constant at 52 degrees Fahrenheit.

Soon they come to the first of many wonders, the Blanket Chamber, where the stalactites resemble handsome silken shawls. The highlight is a huge limestone formation shaped like a blanket, with coloured edges, hanging in folds. Stalactites are the limestone forms growing down from the roof of a cavern, many columnar or pipelike, some as slender as straws, but others of fantastic shapes and groupings. Stalagmites, on the other hand, build up from the floor of the cave, many of them developing in time into solid limestone pillars. Often a stalagmite will join with a stalactite immediately above it, for most stalagmites are formed by the aggregation of countless minute particles of limestone evaporated out of the drippings from a stalactite. Similar evaporation also forms the stalactite, which begins to grow when water, heavily charged with lime, seeps through the roof of a cave.

Other fascinating features in the Waitomo Cave are the Tomo, a vertical shaft in the limestone seventy feet deep; the Banqueting Hall, the Cathedral, and the eight-foot high Organ with its massed hundreds of glistening white columns, considered to be the most imposing single formation of all. Skilfully placed lighting enhances the natural beauty of the features, showing up their colours and the translucent nature of the limestone. Wooden floor walks, handrails, and well-designed stairways make for safe and easy passage among these marvels.

Steps lead down from the Banqueting Hall to the underground Waitomo Stream, where a punt awaits in a vast silent vault beneath the hill. In Stygian darkness the guide shepherds visitors into the boat. Already they have been warned not to speak or make a sound. The punt has no oars and no rowlocks. It is pulled along by the boatman grasping overhead wires.

Soon the noiseless craft rounds a bend — and the watchers catch their breath. The walls and roof of the grotto are seen to glow with light from a myriad minute lanterns, an estimated 100,000 of them. A soft, blue-green radiance illumines this vast chamber a hundred feet long, fifty feet high and forty feet wide. The effect is ethereal. Among the tiny "lamps" hang stalactites;

and encrusting them are fine silken webs spun by the light-givers, for the glow-worms are the larvae of a small fly resembling the "daddy long-legs".

The creators of this unique phantasmagoria are themselves unique. They exist only through a delicate balance between them and their food-supply — tiny midges which hatch in the waters of the stream below. From their webs the glow-worms suspend fairy fishing-lines, studded with sticky globules. Into these the midges fly, and so become trapped. The New Zealand glow-worm (quite different from those of other countries) emits its light from the end segment of its body; but the least noise in the Grotto will cause the tiny tail-light to snuff out.

The other two caves, Ruakuri and Aranui, are a short drive from the Waitomo Hotel. Ruakuri, largest of the three, has an underground river and a hidden waterfall, which, though small, reverberates mightily in the natural echo-chambers of the cavern. The Ruakuri Cave was first explored in 1904 by a settler named James Holden. Its name means "the cave of the dogs", referring to a Maori legend which describes the cavern entrance as once being occupied by wild dogs and their young.

Aranui Cave was not discovered until 1911, when a Maori of that name came upon it when hunting pigs. Aranui is described by J. H. Richards (in *Waitomo Caves*) as the smallest and love-liest of the three caves — the loveliest, that is, in the delicacy and the continuous variety of its stalactites and stalagmites. Aranui, he says, is "pure cave" all the way. Its attraction is ascribed to an almost unending succession of white limestone formations crowding on top of each other in enchanting array.

New Zealand's limestone wonders have not yet been fully explored, and from time to time local speleologists announce new subterranean discoveries. In 1956 a team from Auckland University penetrated deep into the little-known Waituna Cave, west of Te Kuiti, and photographed what is believed to be some of the finest cave scenery in the world.

The Sugar Loaves

In their dying stages volcanoes sometimes have their vents blocked by lava which hardens into a plug or core of exceptional toughness. After aeons of time, when the rest of the mountain has weathered away, this neck, or tholoid, remains as a gigantic monolith towering above the surrounding countryside. One such feature is the "Devil's Thumb" (Mount Tokatoka) near Dargaville, 680 feet high.

Another is the 500-foot Paritutu Rock which overlooks the port of New Plymouth; while scattered in the sea close by are the remarkable Sugar Loaves — a ring of small more-or-less conical islands named by Captain Cook because of their resemblance to loaf sugar, which in those days was often made cone-shaped. Called Ngamotu by the Maoris, the Sugar Loaf Islands probably formed the rim of an ancient volcanic crater, now mostly submerged and eroded.

New Zealand has a number of these tholoids, including the island called Motutaiko which stands off the south-eastern shore of Lake Taupo. In ancient times the Maoris buried their dead on Motutaiko, and some of the burial caves may still be seen there.

"Dicky" Barrett

In the early days a number of European adventurers became involved, some by accident, others by choice, in the Maori tribal wars. Among them were so-called Pakeha-Maoris who became tribal members by marrying Maori women, undergoing tattooing, and adopting Maori customs, sometimes to escape death or slavery at the hands of their Maori captors. Such men were usually runaway convicts from penal settlements in Australia, shipwrecked sailors, or deserters.

One, Kimble Bent, was a renegade soldier who became a Maori slave and, during the wars of the 1860s, fought for the Maoris against the British. Others, such as Captain John Kent, were traders who found it convenient to accept the Maori mode of life. In this group was the brilliant Irishman, F. E. Maning, who became a Judge of the Native Land Court and wrote two notable books, *War in the North* and *Old New Zealand*.

The bay or shore whalers added their quota of picturesque characters, and one, Richard Barrett, had by 1828 established a whaling station at Ngamotu, near the Sugar Loaf Islands, where his grave may still be seen. This occupies a fenced plot in a corner of the once-extensive Ngamotu Pa (now the site of large refrigerated stores) which Barrett and his handful of white whalers more than once helped to defend against the attacks of hostile tribes, especially from the Waikato.

In 1832 about 4,000 Waikato warriors, led by the blood-thirsty Te Whero Whero, who later became the first Maori "King", laid siege to the pa, which was defended by fewer than 400 people. By then Barrett had married Wakaiwa, a chieftainess of the Ngati-te-Whiti tribe, with whom he lived at Ngamotu; so he and his whalers, armed with muskets and a few small cannon, took an active part in the defence.

One of their guns exploded, causing some casualties to the garrison; and, when their shot ran out, they were reduced to firing nails, scraps of iron, and stones from the beach. For three weeks they managed to fend off the attackers, who finally withdrew. But so great was the damage to the morale of the inhabitants, and to their foodcrops, that most of the people, including Barrett, left the Ngamotu area and slipped away south to Waikanae, to be under the protection of powerful allies. Only twenty Maoris were found living in the Ngamotu neighbourhood when its first white settlers arrived in the *William Bryan* in 1841.

While still in his early thirties Barrett became one of Wellington's most notable early citizens, establishing an hotel at Thorndon, near the present site of the Wellington Railway Station. This hostelry became the social and political hub of the new settlement. Balls, banquets, stage shows, and levees were all held there, while for years Barretts Hotel housed vice-royalty and politicians. The establishment was wrecked by an earthquake in 1855, eight years after the death of its founder; but another Barretts Hotel now stands on Lambton Quay in the heart of the city.

Many people nowadays remember Barrett's name because of two spectacular shipwrecks occurring on the notorious Barretts Reef — a navigational hazard at the western side of the entrance to Wellington Harbour. In February 1947 the trans-Tasman passenger vessel *Wanganella* went aground there while on her very first post-war voyage. Fine weather and calm seas for the unusual period of a fortnight enabled this ship to be refloated.

Less fortunate, however, was the inter-island ferry *Wahine* which on 10 April 1968, struck the reef during New Zealand's worst recorded hurricane and sank with the loss of fifty-one lives.

Taranaki Oil

At Moturoa, the port area of New Plymouth, is the first and oldest British oilfield. It is, in fact, one of the oldest in the world, and it has a fantastic history.

Early colonists found that when they kicked aside stones on the seashore there, pools formed containing a dark, smelly liquid. Settlers would watch this liquid bubbling up in the sea, together with gas. The Maoris also had noticed this, and ascribed it to an *atua*, or spirit, drowned long ago and still undergoing putrefaction.

Then came news of the world's first oil well, sunk by Edwin Drake in America, and the New Plymouth colonists scented profit in this smelly stuff which was messing up their beaches.

In 1865 a member of the local legislature, Mr E. M. Smith (nick-named "Ironsand Smith" because of his determined efforts to promote another Taranaki industry based on the local ferriferous beach-sands) sent a sample of Moturoa oil to the Birmingham Chemical Association, England. He received a very favourable report; so he encouraged a namesake, called "Tinker" Smith, because of his vaunted engineering skill, to form a small company to hunt out this oil.

They began to dig for it — with shovels, in the sand! Incredible though it sounds today, when oilmen often prospect for years and spend millions of pounds before getting a "strike", these optimists, with no capital worth talking about, only the crudest gear, and not a shred of technical experience or backing, actually struck oil at their very first try.

Twenty feet down, the diggers encountered gas in such quantities that they were unable to work in it. One man collapsed and was taken to hospital. That was in January, 1866 — the same year as the famous "strike" at Pithole, USA, where a town of 15,000 sprang up in a few months from a single farmhouse.

To ventilate their shaft the Taranaki entrepreneurs rigged up a wind-sail, and burrowed on. By 17 March their well was down to sixty feet, and small quantities of oil were being obtained. The local newspaper reported at the time: "This oil is thick and of a greenish brown colour. It has the genuine oil smell, but not so strong as the purified oil."

The elated prospectors then erected a derrick, and began to drill. They slapped up a notice reading: "To Oil, or London" — indicating their readiness to bore clean through the earth.

This well, which they called the Alpha, and others sunk about the same time, were soon abandoned after reaching a maximum production of some eighty gallons a day, from levels around 100 feet. But the hunt was on; company after company "tried its arm" in this promising area, some wells yielding mineral water, others brine, others again exploding or catching fire when oil-gas ignited. But sufficient high-grade petroleum was won to have the Moturoa field classified as a producer on world oil maps; and today it is still producing steadily both gas and oil in small but marketable quantities.

By 1910 so much crude oil was stored in underground tanks near New Plymouth that its owners did not know what to do with it. For at that time they had no refinery, no local market, and no means of export. A government locomotive adapted to burn the crude oil pulled heavy loads. An account of a trial run from New Plymouth to Wellington says: "The trial seemed to be quite satisfactory apart from the smoke and the smell trailing over the landscape.

"It was noteworthy and comical to see how other railwaymen took the passage of the consumer of Taranaki oil. Some raised their hats ironically to us, and with the other hand held their noses."

Overseas experts have always shown a lively interest in this Taranaki field, and during recent years some of the world's biggest oil combines have spent vast sums on surveying and drilling both there and in other parts of New Zealand.

In 1938, for example, one group began boring at Totangi, near Gisborne, with equipment of the latest type brought from America. They sank eight wells, including one at Midhirst in Taranaki which went down 10,925 feet. During World War II another powerful group of companies operated near Marton, further inland.

Yet for all their outlay, and with personnel and equipment capable of dealing with any known drilling porblem, they found no oil.

Meanwhile the Moturoa locals soldiered on. In 1931 two new bores, sunk to the 2,200 feet level, proved to be steady producers. So a small locally-built refinery — the smallest in the commonwealth, probably in the world — was erected to cope with their output and that of two or three other wells which "came in" later. Some other wells in this area yielded petroleum gas, which was piped into the city supply at New Plymouth, four miles away.

This first Moturoa refinery, which cost only a few thousand pounds to build, never ceased to operate because of a shortage of oil. Its earlier products, though limited in range, and small in quantity, always found a ready local market.

But the Taranaki field still awaited a full-scale scientific quest for the major oil reservoirs always believed to lie there somewhere at some level, beneath forest or farmland, or even under the sea. Such a quest began in 1955 when a consortium known as Shell-BP-Todd Oil Services Ltd gained exploration rights and assembled a forty-seven man team which included a number of the world's top geophysical experts.

After three years of intensive work, which included a seismic probe right around the base of Mount Egmont, the company selected a site for its first well — on the Palmer Road, Kapuni, a farming settlement sixteen miles from the Taranaki coast, and forty-six miles south by road from Moturoa.

Drilling began there on 27 January 1959, and four months later this Kapuni No. 1 well was down to 11,000 feet. The company had spent over a million pounds, and all they had got, one official said, was a deep hole.

Dourly they drilled on, to 13,000 feet. Then a halt was called, for testing at various levels in the well. This resulted in an outburst of gas which continued to flow at considerable pressure and in encouraging volume. Quantities of condensate (a light oil) were also obtained. The Kapuni site had proved a winner.

After drilling in various other places, including the East

Coast of the North Island, the consortium "settled down" to develop the Kapuni field, sinking further wells, with results which have now justified the outlay of some twelve million dollars, and the company's enormous faith and determination. Today, natural gas from this field is being piped to a number of New Zealand towns and cities, including Wellington and Auckland where the supply commenced in March 1970. Oil from Kapuni is shipped via New Plymouth to the $40,000,000 refinery (built earlier for treating imported petroleum) at Whangarei.

But the epic story of Taranaki oil, now more than 100 years old, did not end at Kapuni. The Shell-BP-Todd consortium moved their search out to sea where, not far from the Taranaki coast, they discovered a new field, the Maui, which proved to have reserves of gas and condensate many times greater than those of the Kapuni field. Some crude oil too was found, but insufficient to justify its exploitation without the commercial usage of Maui's gas and condensates. These Taranaki successes have served to intensify oil search activities elsewhere in New Zealand, including other offshore areas, so this country may well be entering an "oil boom" phase which will have incalculable effects on its economy.

The Raurimu Spiral

New Zealand engineers faced some knotty problems, including the opposition of hostile Maoris, when constructing the Main Trunk Railway from Auckland to Wellington. In thirty-one miles of country south of Taumarunui the railway climbs 2,086 feet to National Park, the steepest part being over the mountain range which rises immediately behind the Raurimu station, 199 miles from Auckland.

There the line begins an ascent of 714 feet, to surmount which it was laid in the form of an ascending spiral — a complete circle, and two loops, one of them shaped like a very long horseshoe. In this loop, after travelling only one mile from Raurimu, the line doubles back to within 300 feet of its starting point. It has then climbed eighty-two vertical feet.

Next comes the Spiral itself with its two tunnels, of nineteen chains and four and a half chains. At one and three-quarter miles from Raurimu the line passes over the first tunnel, seventy-four feet below. At that point the line has climbed 232 feet. Half a mile further on it has almost completed a circle only eighteen chains in diameter; and at three miles by rail from Raurimu it is still only three-quarters of a mile away in a direct line. At its fourth mile the line has ascended more than 400 feet.

This remarkable piece of engineering, designed by Mr R. W. Holmes, and involving a grade of one-in-fifty on the Spiral itself, was opened to traffic on 6 November 1908.

North Island Miscellany

Beside the main highway near Atiamuri, in the Wairakei area, is the curious Hatupatu Rock. Shaped like a small bell-tent, this rock is hollow, and has a "door" or opening. According to Maori legend the rock was once solid, but on the uttering of the proper incantation it opened to admit a young man named Hatupatu, who was being pursued by an evil spirit.

Lake in a Lake

New Zealand has examples of a lake on an island within a lake. The beautiful Lake Waikare-iti, in the East Coast district of the North Island, contains several islets; and one, called Rahui, has its own tiny lake upon it. Waikare-iti acts a feeder for yet another lake, the exquisite and much larger Waikare-moana, some 2,000 feet below.

Longest Place-Name

It would take a better man than most to pronounce New Zealand's longest place-name:

TAUMATAWHAKATANGIHANGAKOAUAU
OTAMATEAPOKAIWHENUAKITANATAHU!

This is the official title of an 890-foot hill near Porangahau in Hawke's Bay. A literal translation of the name would be: "The summit where Tamatea-pokai-whenua (Tamatea the circumnavigator) played his flute to his beloved". It is three letters longer than the Welsh name once claimed to be the longest in the world.

Spas and Hot Springs

Spas where people may bathe in the soothing or curative waters of hot mineral springs have been developed at a number of places in New Zealand. Among the Northland spas are Helensville, thirty-eight miles north of Auckland; Waiwera, twenty-eight miles north on the east coast, where a fine resort with modern hotel and other facilities has been developed amid idyllic coastal scenery; Kamo, about four miles north of Whangarei, and Ngawha, in the far north.

Of these the most remarkable in some ways is Ngawha, between Kaikohe and Ohaeawai, where a thermal area of about eight square miles still remains largely undeveloped. There one finds the same sulphur smells, hot pools, wisps of rising steam and brittle mud-crust underfoot as at Rotorua.

The ground through which the hot water and gases rise contains globules of free mercury, and Ngawha is thus claimed to have the only natural mercury baths in the world. Other minerals occur in the muds and pools at Ngawha, where sufferers go to seek relief for skin ailments and such complaints as rheumatism and sciatica. A number of people, mostly aged, live permanently in the small settlement there, while casual visitors can find accommodation either in the private hotel built right at the Springs, or in licensed hotels only a few miles distant on the main highway.

South of Auckland thermal springs are even more numerous. Outside the extensive Rotorua-Wairakei-Taupo system, spas have been developed at various places, all popular as holiday resorts, and for the therapeutic value of the waters. The largest is at Te Aroha, an attractive inland town of some 3,000 people about thirty-four miles north-east from Hamilton by road or rail, and the same distance south-east from Thames. Te Aroha has both licensed and private hotels, and a delightful Hot Springs Domain controlled by the New Zealand Tourist Department. Covering about twenty acres, this Domain includes public bath buildings, tennis courts, bowling and croquet greens, in most attractive surroundings. Te Aroha also has a golf links, a racecourse, and private bathing facilities with individual bathrooms. The waters of this spa contain sodium bicarbonate and are similar to but stronger than those of the famous Vichy resort in France. They are used for the relief of rheumatism, dyspepsia and other internal disorders, while they also make a refreshing drink when lemon or other flavouring is added.

On the coast due east from Te Aroha is Katikati, which has a licensed hotel and, at a short distance from the township, thermal springs with hot mineral baths. Katikati is linked by road with Tauranga, a noted seaside resort about twenty-five miles further south.

Waingaro, north-west from Hamilton and due west from Ngaruawahia, has a licensed hotel and other facilities near which a large spring discharges mineral water at a temperature of 130 degrees Fahrenheit.

Due east from Hamilton, at a road and rail distance of forty-eight and thirty-six miles respectively, is Matamata, a townlet of some 2,000 people, with hot springs set in beautiful rural surroundings. This spa has bathing pools, a well-appointed motor camp and a children's playground. Thirteen miles further south at Okoroire are more thermal baths, close to a golf course, motor camp and a licensed hotel. On the west coast, near Kawhia, are thermal springs which arise in the sands of the beach, like the ones already mentioned near Whitianga, on the east coast.

Tokaanu, at the southern end of Lake Taupo, provides not only hot springs but fishing, hunting, boating, bathing, climbing and a variety of thermal attractions. Included are geysers, boiling mudpools, and quiescent volcanoes, one of which, Pihanga (4,352 feet) has a crater lake. At Tokaanu is a modern hotel controlled by the New Zealand Tourist Hotel Corporation. The hotel has natural hot water laid on, and its own natural hot pool outside. Nearby a public bath-house has been built in an attractive domain.

Other noted North Island springs are at Te Puia and Morere, respectively north and south of Gisborne, each with a licensed hotel. At both these spas, naturally occurring chemical substances, including iodine, attractively tint the water.

CHAPTER SIXTEEN

South Island Features

The Southern Alps

Because of its mountains New Zealand has been called the "Switzerland of the South". But New Zealand's Southern Alps alone are much greater in extent than the whole of Switzerland, and cover probably twice that country's area. Like a vast backbone down the middle of the South Island, this mighty range, with its peaks and its spurs, its glaciers, lakes and snowfields, provides an unrivalled alpine playground, unique for its accessibility and for the variety of its attractions. Alpine conditions in New Zealand begin lower than in most other countries, while the permanent snowline is 3,000 feet lower than in Switzerland.

In the New Zealand Alps one may climb, hike, ski; skate on the frozen lakes; fish for trout or salmon; hunt chamois, tahr, or red deer. The main range has seventeen peaks of over 10,000 feet, topped by Mt Cook, 12,349 feet, known to the Maori as Aorangi, "the Cloud Piercer". Several passes have been found through the mountains, and one of these, Arthur's Pass, is traversed by road and railway, amid magnificent scenery. In the heart of the Mt Cook Alpine region is the luxurious Hermitage Lodge, situated 2,510 feet above sea level. This alpine resort hotel can be reached through regular transport services, both by land and by air, which ply from Christchurch, Dunedin and Invercargill.

Ski-planes also serve the area, and will land sightseers on the glaciers 7,000 feet above sea level where extensive snowfields, unobstructed by trees or rocks, provide excellent skiing at all times of the year. These planes, and those on regular schedule over the roof of New Zealand's alpine wonderland, provide a thousand thrills for their passengers as they weave in and out among peaks and chasms.

"The Organ", Waitomo Caves.

The entrance portico to the Glow-worm Grotto, Waitomo Caves.

The world's longest place name, Hawke's Bay, North Island.

TAUMATAWHAKA-
TANGIHANGAKOAUAU-
ATAMATEAPOKAI-
WHENUAKITANATAHU.

With a cruising height of 8,000 feet, amid mountains rising to ten or twelve thousand, the pilots must skim the tops of some peaks, twist around others. They shoot through gaps between them, zooming up steep gorges on one side, down them on the other. And since distances are deceptive in such terrain, pilots and passengers seem to be constantly dodging death by inches.

The Glaciers

The glaciers of the Southern Alps comprise an extensive system in which some flow eastward, others to the west. More than 360 glaciers have been named, and they cover a total area of 330 square miles. All occur between latitudes 43 degrees and 45 degrees South.

Those on the eastern slopes of the Divide are slower-moving, the largest being the Tasman Glacier, seventeen and a half miles long and one and a quarter miles wide; the Murchison, nine miles; the Mueller, eight miles; the Godley and the Hooker each six and a half miles long. All five drain into the Waitaki River system.

On the western slopes the glaciers are more numerous because of greater snowfalls, and they descend to lower levels. Since the western slopes are steeper, their glaciers also flow more quickly. Two of them, the Fox and the Franz Josef, are served by tourist hotels and other facilities. A road distance of only fifteen miles separates these two glaciers, and both are unusual in that their lower reaches flow through dense, evergreen rainforest, against which the white ice-cliffs of their terminal faces make a remarkable contrast. Both the Fox and the Franz Josef peter out quite near the sea, and less than 1000 feet above it; so these two glaciers are by far the world's most accessible. Each year they attract thousands of visitors, many of whom are mountaineers using the glaciers as access routes to the towering peaks of the Southern Alps, or as starting places for transalpine visits to the Hermitage on the eastern side of the Divide.

From a starting point 8,000 feet up, the Fox Glacier flows eight and a half miles, and the Franz Josef seven miles — a gradient of about 1000 feet to the mile. The Franz Josef ends in an ice-cliff half a mile wide and 100 feet high. Measurements made of the surface speed of this glacier indicate exceptionally high rates of flow, ranging from 100 to 200 inches a day, as close as two miles from the terminus, contrasting with the Tasman glacier on the eastern side which travels only about twenty inches daily at a point seven miles upstream.

On the western side of the Southern Alps there is also the unique Balfour Glacier, which has two sections — an upper one ending in a spectacular icefall from the brink of a precipice, and a lower one which continues on from the icefall. A remarkable feature of the glaciers ending near the west coast is the recent retreat of their terminal face, in some cases by more than half a mile, in the past twelve or fifteen years. Both the Fox and the Franz Josef have hot springs in their neighbourhood, while visitors to either glacier can make side trips to some of the numerous bush-girt lakes remarkable for their reflections of vast snowy mountains.

Milford Sound

Haakon Mielche writes in his book *Round the World with the Galathea* that he is sorry for anyone who has to go to his grave without seeing Milford Sound.

"It is," he asserts (and as a Scandinavian he should know), "a fiord wider and more beautiful than the famous ones of Norway. It lay filled with sunlight, the air spiced with the scent of the thick bushes on shore. Trees clung to the rock where there was the least hold for their roots. Little paradise ducks were paddling along the coast, the glens were buzzing with summer insects, chaffinches were chirruping, and the song of the blackbirds mingled with the tinkling notes of the bellbirds." An idyllic picture! And anyone who has not walked the famed Milford Track has indeed missed the experience of a lifetime.

Milford is a true "fiord" — the word meaning a threshold — with a head of immense depth, but considerably shallower at the seaward end. There the ancient glacier which gouged out the basin began to melt and deposit its moraine — masses of rock and debris which glaciers carry embedded in their ice. But the entrance to Milford is still deep enough to allow the passage of the largest ocean-going vessels, some of which take tourists there while on world or Pacific cruises.

In a ten-mile voyage up Milford Sound several glaciers are sighted, the finest being the Pembroke, on a mountain of the same name, which towers above the water to a height of 6,710 feet.

Mitre Peak

Another renowned feature in the Milford area is Mitre Peak, named because of its likeness to a bishop's head-dress. Though appearing from most angles as a single peak, the summit of this mountain, which rises from the water to a height of 5,560 feet, actually comprises five separate pinnacles. Clearly visible in its entirety from the windows of the fine Milford Hotel, Mitre Peak is one of the world's most photographed mountains.

Sutherland Falls

In the same area and equally photogenic are the Sutherland Falls, New Zealand's highest cascades. Here the water leaps in three spectacular flights, to fall a vertical distance of 1,904 feet. The longest cascade is the top one, of 815 feet; next biggest is the middle drop of 751 feet.

Although this is the largest waterfall in New Zealand, on a world scale it is outclassed by several others, for example the Angel Falls of Venezuela — the world's highest — which drop 3,212 feet.

New Zealand's Browne Falls, which spill out from Browne Lake to descend the south-western side of Malaspina Sound, are about 2,500 feet in height. But as Dollimore observes in *The New Zealand Guide*, although designated a waterfall, Browne Falls are more in the nature of a steep cataracting stream or a "water-slide".

Te Ana-au Caves

Another glow-worm grotto, rivalling the North Island's Waitomo, has been discovered and opened for tourists on the shores of Lake Te Anau. In April 1947, Lawson Burrows, an operator of launch tourist services on the lake, found this cave, which had been described in ancient Maori legend but was otherwise unknown.

The cave is close to the lake-shore and provides passage for a stream flowing from Lake Orbell in a valley high above — a valley which is the home of that rare bird the notornis. Burrows followed the waters upward through underground lakes, whirlpools and waterfalls and finally ventured into a subterranean grotto similar to the celebrated one at Waitomo. Working under extraordinary difficulties, the discoverer has since developed his grotto — building stairways, duck-walks, and so on — until it has become an outstanding tourist attraction.

Te Anau, the name of New Zealand's second largest lake, is a contraction of Te Ana-au, meaning "a cave of swirling waters". This had puzzled researchers for years, since no cave was known to exist there. Lawson Burrows' discovery cleared this mystery, and he also revealed the existence of not just one cave but a whole series.

Wakatipu: A Lake that Breathes

Best-known of the southern alpine lakes is Wakatipu, which occupies a glacial trench forty-eight miles long and up to three miles wide. Bordered on all sides by majestic mountains, many of which have glaciers, Wakatipu has been called "New Zealand's Lucerne". With its surface at an altitude of 1,017 feet and a maximum depth of 1,239 feet, this lake extends 222 feet below sealevel.

A fascinating and baffling feature of Wakatipu is its "breathing" — the regular rise and fall of the waters, averaging three inches every fifteen minutes. Maori legend attributes this to the respirations of a goblin or monster inhabiting the depths, an interesting if unacceptable theory. Sheep-farming and cattle-raising are well-established occupations in areas around the lake, and a number of settlements have been formed, some more than 100 years ago.

In 1862 the discovery of gold along the Shotover River near Lake Wakatipu caused a minor boom for some of these settlements, especially Queenstown, which quickly became the main supply source and point of entry for the diggings. The lake provided the principal means of transportation, and in less than a year its fleet had grown from one whaleboat owned by a pioneer settler to four steamers and about thirty other craft.

Today Queenstown is a thriving tourist centre nestling beneath the mighty rampart of the Remarkable Range (8,880 feet) and giving access to first-class skiing on nearby Coronet Peak. It has an airport, a hospital, modern shops, hotels and motels, and regular motor services to such places as Mt Cook, the other southern lakes, the city of Christchurch, and to railways which end at Invercargill and Dunedin. A twin-screw steamer, a hydrofoil, and a fleet of launches make scheduled trips to places of the interest around the lake, including a sanctuary for paradise duck and a high country sheep station. There visitors may take tea in a large stone homestead more than 100 years old (but furnished in the modern style) before wandering off to ride the range or shear a sheep.

In the delightful public gardens at Queenstown a large natural boulder, surrounded by a bed of deep blue forget-me-nots, honours the memory of Captain Robert Falcon Scott, RN, the noted Antarctic explorer. Attached to the stone is a simple plaque bearing a transcript of Scott's last journal entry.

The Southern Springs

Besides the hot springs in the Fox and Franz Josef areas there are others in the South Island at Maruia and Hanmer, both of which have become noted health resorts. The development of the Hanmer Springs was begun by the New Zealand Government in the early 1900s and the spa now has well-appointed bath buildings, hotels and guest-houses, an extensive motor camp and a range of recreational facilities including an eighteen-hole golf course.

In a sheltered locale 1,220 feet up, the Hanmer Springs sanatorium (now Queen Mary Hospital) has become a first-class centre for the treatment of nervous disorders. It has helped to rehabilitate thousands of sufferers, including large numbers of ex-servicemen and women. The waters at Hanmer are bland and antiseptic, the climate is bracing, the air pure and dust-free. Natural gas (methane) comes up at the site of the springs and is stored in a gasometer for a limited use in heating and cooking.

Largest Fresh-Water Springs

The Waikoropupu Springs, near Takaka in the Nelson Province, are claimed to be the largest fresh-water springs in the world. There an underground river gushes to the surface through cracks in the prevailing limestone, pouring forth 475,000,000 gallons of water every twenty-four hours. This rate never varies. The name is shortened locally to Pupu Springs.

South Island Miscellany

Most districts in New Zealand have some curious natural feature which is unique to this country though it may be duplicated within it. Examples in the South Island are the petrified forests on the beach at Curio Bay, Southland; the Marble Mountain, near Takaka, in the Nelson Province, with its white slabs and outcrops resembling a vast graveyard; and the Moeraki Boulders, geological curiosities known as septarians, which are found on the Moeraki Beach on the east coast of Otago between Oamaru and Dunedin. These boulders comprise thousands of stone spheres, ranging in size from that of a cricket ball to a wartime floating mine. Their interiors are red or yellow, their centres crystalline.

Equally unusual are the Pancake Rocks at Punakaiki, between the West Coast towns of Greymouth and Westport. There a headland of stratified limestone has been weathered and eroded to look like huge piles of pancakes. Sea water rushes through caverns in the cliffs, making ominous roars and rumblings, and if wind and tide conditions are right, spouting up through blowholes in a spectacular display.

Another geological oddity is the Red Mountain of northwest Otago, which can be seen from ships at sea. Red Mountain has been described as "a huge intrusion of peridotite rock which in an ancient geological age thrust itself upwards, bursting between the overlying schists". So now we know! Since the rock contains much iron ore it is covered with red oxide, a product of weathering, and no vegetation will grow upon it.

The Marlborough Sounds

At the north-eastern end of the South Island these sounds, with their innumerable arms branching and re-branching, make a maze of natural waterways so intricate that only a large-scale map could represent them in all their detail. They comprise about 1000 square miles of water, mostly in sunken valleys which the sea has invaded.

The two main inlets are Pelorus Sound, named after a British warship which anchored there in 1838, and Queen Charlotte Sound, which Captain Cook named in honour of the wife of his sovereign, George III, in 1770. Both these sounds are entered from Cook Strait, a notoriously stormy stretch of water whose gales seldom disturb the serenity of the innumerable land-locked havens provided by the vast Marlborough Sounds complex.

Across Cook Strait is the capital city, Wellington, only a few hours away by sea, a matter of minutes by plane. Modern drive-on ferries make frequent scheduled trips — three each way on most days — between Wellington and Picton, the South Island's "front door", at the head of Queen Charlotte Sound. A pleasant well-found holiday resort, Picton is also the terminus of the South Island's Main Trunk Railway, and it gives access to an extensive system of highways encompassing the whole island.

Thus Picton has become the mecca for thousands of holiday-makers who each year use as their playground the many hundred miles of placid waters which wind and branch among the bush-clad slopes of sheltering hills. There people of all ages tramp, shoot, fish, or ramble through the forest. Others enjoy yachting, water skiing, speedboat racing, rowing. Thirty kinds of fish can be caught in the Marlborough Sounds, and amateurs often catch dozens in a day. Commercial fishermen net heavy harvests, their catches once ranging from sprats to whales, for Tory Channel, which connects Queen Charlotte Sound with Cook Strait, was until quite recent times the venue of a vigorous shore-based whaling industry, first established in the late 1820s.

Daffy Dolphins

In the late 1880s great interest centred on the Marlborough Sounds because of the activities of a Risso's dolphin which became so famous that songs were written about it, and people from abroad, including the noted writer Frank T. Bullen, travelled to Nelson especially to see it. A motion picture (one of the earliest) was made of this dolphin, and a special law was passed for its protection.

For twenty-four years, from 1888 to 1912, Pelorus Jack, as the dolphin was called, met and escorted ships crossing Admiralty Bay on the regular route between Nelson and Wellington. In that time thousands of travellers making the crossing were intrigued and entertained by the cavortings of this playful fellow which, it is said, never missed a steamer traversing the route.

Though sometimes fired at by feckless voyagers, Pelorus Jack lived out a normal dolphin life-span and probably died of sheer old age . . . a different ending from that of Opo, an equally remarkable dolphin whose antics drew huge crowds to the little North Island township of Opononi throughout the summer of 1955-56.

From following and frolicking around small boats, holding up her throat to be scratched by oars, and generalyy displaying a playful amiability, Opo progressed to an active fraternisation with certain children — selected, apparently, for their gentleness and compatibility. These Opo allowed to stroke, scratch and tickle her and smaller children sometimes rode upon her back.

Opo soon learned to do many tricks with beach ball and bottle, flipping them aloft with tail or snout, to the delight of great crowds of onlookers. She also joined in water games with groups of children, persistently seeking human company in a manner not recorded for a wild dolphin since the first century AD.

Opo also gained special protection, first from a local committee, which erected notices requesting care in dealing with her; then by an Order-in-Council due to take effect at midnight of 8 March 1956. But the next day Opo was found dead, jammed in a rock crevice, and presumed to have been stunned by a gelignite explosion.

Sorrow spread throughout the land. Opo was honoured with a flower-laden grave in the Opononi township, and the Governor-General sent a telegram of sympathy to the children there. A leading New Zealand sculptor carved and donated a work in Hinuera stone depicting a boy and a dolphin; and this now stands as a permanent memorial to a brief but happy episode which stirred the hearts of a nation.

Lake Matheson, Westland, with the Southern Alps in the distance.

Terminal of the Franz Josef Glacier, Westland.

Pancake Rocks at Punakaiki, on the West Coast of the South Island.

Moeraki Boulders, Otago, South Island.

Auckland Harbour Bridge by night.

CHAPTER SEVENTEEN

From Pole to Equator

THEORETICALLY NEW ZEALAND'S jurisdiction extended until quite lately from the tiny, twelve-square-mile atoll of Nauru (mostly phosphate) one-half degree south of the Equator, to the 175,000 square mile Ross Dependency (mostly ice) which ends at the South Pole.

After World War I Nauru became a Mandated Territory under the League of Nations, to be "administered jointly by Britain, Australia and New Zealand". A similar arrangement was made after World War II, but in both instances the administration was carried out entirely by Australia. In 1968 this island (total population 6,000) was granted self-government.

Though only a speck in the vast Pacific, Nauru is highly important to both New Zealand and Australia as their main supply-source for phosphate rock, upon which depend "those green pastures" and a substantial proportion of the national wealth.

Equally odd is New Zealand's "administration" of the icy Ross Dependency — a territory with no permanent population (except penguins, seals and seagulls) — a territory, in fact, where the winds blow harder and the temperatures drop lower than at any other place on earth; where no rain falls and where the land is drier than the deserts of Africa, Australia, or America. Even the snow and ice rarely melt there in the normal way, by changing first to liquid. Instead, this solid water, which covers most of the continent to a depth of two miles, passes directly into the air, as water vapour, by a process of sublimation.

On 30 July 1923 the British Government proclaimed by Order-in-Council that "that part of His Majesty's Dominions in the Antarctic Seas which comprises all the islands and territories between the 160th degree of East Longitude and the 150th degree of West Longitude which are situated south of the

60th degree of South latitude shall be named the Ross Dependency". And the Governor-General of New Zealand was appointed as Governor of the territory.

But while New Zealand is held responsible for the "administration" of this sector of Antarctica, no country can claim ownership to any part of it. This was agreed by the Antarctic Treaty of 1959; and among the various nationals now engaged there on a wide range of scientific enterprises (to which New Zealand is making a small but effective contribution) there is much cordiality and goodwill. This is specially marked between the New Zealanders and the Americans, some of whose bases lie inside the New Zealand sector. Furthermore, the New Zealand mainland is used by America for the coming and going of its Antarctic personnel, whose giant aircraft arrive at and take off from the Harewood international Airport near Christchurch. In past eras Lyttelton, the port of Christchurch, has also been used as a base and departure point for such Antarctic explorers as Scott, Shackleton, and Sir James Clarke Ross, for whom the New Zealand Dependency was named.

Most famous New Zealander to engage in Antarctic exploration was Sir Edmund Hillary who, with Sherpa Tensing, made the world's first conquest of Mount Everest in May 1953. In December 1956 Hillary led a New Zealand expedition planned, among other enterprises, to link with a British party under Sir Vivian Fuchs in an attempt to make a complete crossing of the Antarctic Continent — an idea first conceived, and attempted unsuccessfully, by Shackleton in 1914-15.

It was Sir Edmund Hillary who established New Zealand's Scott Base and, using motor vehicles, completed the first overland journey from that base to the South Pole.

The Cook Islands

This sunny territory, comprising fifteen Pacific islands with a total land area of less than 100 square miles, (barely sufficient to sustain its population of some 20,000), is scattered over 850,000 square miles of ocean. Yet from 1901, when these islands were declared to lie within the boundaries of New Zealand, until 1965 when the Cooks achieved internal self-government, their administration was the sole responsibility of New Zealand.

New Zealand also undertook the administration of Niue Island and the Tokelaus (eight and a half degrees south of the Equator) the three then comprising the "Island Territories of New Zealand", with their own special Government department, based on Wellington.

According to New Zealand law all native-born residents of these islands have the status of New Zealanders, with unrestricted right of entry to the "mainland". Virtually all are Polynesians, whose native language is very much like that of the New Zealand Maori.

Cook Islanders subsist mainly by fishing, gathering mother-of-pearl shell, drying copra, and growing crops of citrus fruits, pineapples, bananas and tomatoes, marketed mostly in New Zealand.

In recent years small industries have developed in the Cooks for the manufacture of clothing and a range of island curios. In 1965 this group achieved internal self-government, although it is still classified as New Zealand territory overseas, and still depends upon New Zealand for defence and financial support.

Not so long ago the liquor laws for Rarotonga, the main island of the Cook group, were even more curious than those of New Zealand at that time. The one hotel there was unlicensed, so the thirsty traveller or resident whose ideas ranged beyond lemonade or coconut milk was obliged to obtain a medical prescription from the local hospital. Later this was changed, and a police permit was required! More recently the Cook Islands Treasury Department has temptingly advertised the wide range of "goods" in its liquor store, at prices which set New Zealand hearts yearning.

CHAPTER EIGHTEEN

New Zealand Souvenirs

THERE WAS A TIME when dried human heads were eagerly sought as curios by visitors to New Zealand. Museums in Europe, and some private collectors, would pay up to fifty pounds each for such "objets d'art", preferring of course faces which were heavily tattooed.

Supplies, at first, were not hard to come by, since the Maori had a custom of decorating the palisades of his pa with the heads of enemies slain in battle, which he preserved by a process of steaming, smoking, and oiling. With the advent of Europeans, these heads became valuable items of trade, and moves followed to step up the supply.

Businesslike chiefs, intent on securing more muskets (and hence more victories, bringing more heads to sell) would sometimes line up prisoners of war before intending buyers, who could thus choose their own curios in the raw, and bid for them, as it were, "on the hoof".

The unlucky wearers of the heads so selected (they had ceased to be the rightful owners) were often further favoured by having their faces elaborately tattooed — a treatment usually reserved for chiefs — before they parted company with them. But not all of these head-wearers were appreciative of such honour; and an early writer noted that some prisoners were base enough, after all the trouble their captors had taken, to make off with, and thus steal, their own topknots — a capital felony.

Today your visitor to New Zealand will rarely see a tattooed face, much less will he be able to buy one, dead or alive. He will see, however, innumerable carved replicas, grotesque and amusing, on the many genuine Maori houses still extant; in museums, private collections, and in the numerous shops which deal in native curios.

Probably the most attractive souvenirs will be those fashioned from "greenstone", a type of jade, occurring in New Zealand but by no means common there.

This fascinating stone was the Maori's gold — treasured for its rarity, its beauty, its comparative indestructability. From greenstone the Maori fashioned exquisite ear-drops, pendants, and pins for the cloaks of his "nobility" — for it must be remembered that the social hierarchy of the Maori was, despite his many communal customs, a "tiered" one, headed by an aristocracy and based on a worker-cum-slave majority. Somewhere in between were the tohunga, or priests, who exerted considerable influence.

From greenstone the Maori carved his bizarre hei-tiki (now a national emblem) in the shape of squat caricatures of the human figure, with enlarged head set askew, prominent eyes and protruding tongue.

Because of its natural properties, greenstone was also the Maori's steel, from which he fashioned with infinite patience and skill sharp-edged weapons, adzes, and chisels for carving and tattooing. For greenstone he traded his most prized possessions, fought wars, and made arduous journeys to the few remote spots where this substance was obtainable. And early European visitors found that most Maoris firmly resisted all enticements to part with their greenstone artifacts.

Today this rare stone may not be exported to jewellers or lapidaries in other countries, though for years German craftsmen bought it, worked on it in Fatherland factories, and supplied its country of origin with greenstone curios. Protected by this ban, New Zealanders are now producing their own realistic replicas of the hei-tiki, and a whole range of greenstone artifacts — brooches, cuff-links, pendants, eardrops — which the visitor may purchase in most towns and cities.

Modern craftsmen, of course, use electrically-driven diamond drills and saws to fashion their material. The Maori's only aids were sandstone and water, sea shells, and primitive hand drills tipped with quartz or obsidian — a kind of volcanic glass. Greenstone does not flake like other rocks when struck, and so it must be cut, formerly at the expense of infinite time and labour, along the trend of its "grain". After this cutting, Maori craftsmen would spend months, sometimes years, on polishing, first with abrasives such as sand and water, then achieving their characteristic high finish by rubbing the stone on human skin, usually of the thigh or of the stomach.

There are several varieties of New Zealand jade, displaying about twenty different shades. Most prized by the Maori were the kahurangi, a mottled stone of light and dark green; the translucent kawakawa ("into which the eye can look deeply as though into clear water"), with markings like leaves of the kawakawa tree; and the tangiwai, or "tear water", which has its dark green colour patterned with lighter hues in the shape of human tear-drops.

While most New Zealand greenstone consists of nephrite, a mineral varying in colour from whitish to dark green and almost black, the softer and more translucent tangiwai is bowenite, found in the Milford Sound area. Nephrite occurs in the rugged valley of the Arahura River, on the west coast of the South Island.

Recently Dr G. B. Orbell of Invercargill discovered substantial quantities of greenstone, with some boulders estimated at up to six tons, in the Lake Wakatipu area of Central Otago. He located this outcrop by following the clues of ancient Maori stories, which tell of greenstone being obtained from "near a lake, ten days' march from the Waitaki River".

The Paua

A shellfish that is distinctively New Zealand, but related to the abalones of America and similar fish elsewhere, is the paua, mentioned in an earlier chapter.

Its scientific name, *Haliotis iris*, means "rainbow-coloured sea-ear", and refers to the beautiful inner surface of the shell, predominantly silver, but glowing with fiery iridescent tints of green and blue. This brilliant colouring is said to be caused by microgrooves, several thousand to the inch, and so fine as to be imperceptible by touch. The grooves split up the light reflected from the paua shell in much the same way that light is split by water vapour to make a rainbow.

Paua shell — sometimes called New Zealand opal — was often used by the Maori to inlay his woodcarving. Modern craftsmen set it in silver to make jewellery; and they, too, inlay the shell to make a wide range of distinctively beautiful objects, such as trays, caskets and toilet accessories. All these can be bought in New Zealand towns and cities, and increasing quantities are being exported. It is now illegal to export un-worked paua shell, while the meat also must be processed before it can be sold abroad.

Although the smooth and brilliant inner surface of the paua shell commands admiration, this is not the part which modern craftsmen use. They work instead on the rough outer surface, which is quite unattractive, being drab in colour and usually encrusted with the calcareous remains of passenger organisms. These are ground away to reveal a hidden surface of even better quality than the inner one.

CHAPTER NINETEEN

The New Zealand Rockhound

Gold

While most minerals and a wide range of gemstones are found in New Zealand, rock-hunting as a popular hobby has developed only recently. Prospecting of the more serious kind, i.e. with an eye to commercial wealth, has on the other hand, quite a long history.

Gold undoubtedly is the best example, with the local gold-rushes of the 1860s bearing comparison with those of Alaska, California and Australia. Rip-roaring times were those, when pay-dirt worth $50 could be won by a fossicker between dawn and sunset; when two mates collected 300 ounces (worth then about $8 an ounce) in one day; when two others rode into the town of Dunedin carrying no less than eighty-seven pounds weight of gold worth about $12,000.

Men then poured into the country at the rate of 1000 a day. Bread cost $1 a loaf, flour between 30 and 40 cents a pound. Mushroom settlements and canvas towns sprang up — for example Hokitika, which in two years grew from a single store to a conglomeration of ramshackle dwellings housing some 50,000 people, and 100 hotels. The population of Hokitika toay is only about 3,000.

Over the years, more than 27,000,000 ounces of gold have been exported from New Zealand, worth about $350 million dollars. One mine alone, the Martha in the North Island, had, when it closed in 1952, produced gold and silver worth $56,992,022. Its first owner sold it, in 1890, for $3,000 — a fortune in those days, but only a speck compared with what he might have had!

One unique development on the New Zealand goldfields was the introduction of bucket dredges, the first being the steam-driven *Dunedin*, built in 1886. These distinctive craft operated on the rivers of Otago, Southland and Westland, reaching peak numbers in 1903 when 264 were at work. Today the sole survivor is the dredge *Kaniere* at Kumara, a township in Westland which now has a population of only a few hundred, but which in 1876 boasted eighty hotels, a daily paper, and a School of Mines. It was here, incidentally, that one of New Zealand's most colourful and dynamic political personalities, Richard John Seddon, began his career, as a storekeeper. As Prime Minister from 1893 to 1906 he initiated much of the advanced social legislation for which New Zealand is noted.

Little gold is now won in New Zealand, although in the South Island tourists and visitors are often taken for tours of the old "diggings", allowed to inspect small sluicing installations, and invited to "pan a dish of dirt". In this way many people are still able to take home real gold which they have wrested themselves from Mother Earth. But their chances of finding a rich lode, valuable "pay dirt", or even a decent-sized nugget, are slim.

Precious Stones

In many areas the New Zealand rockhound can still find chunks of gold-specked quartz; or he can win grains of the pure metal by panning certain beach sands and river gravels. People on the South Island's west coast find this quite a profitable hobby, especially after storms and heavy seas. Diamonds and emeralds have not yet appeared on the New Zealand mineral map, nor is the New Zealand oyster noted for yielding pearls. Its function is essentially gastronomic.

But if he bounds off, equipped with knapsack, pick, and hammer, to the high hills and gorges, or follows in the footsteps of some practised prospector, the New Zealand rockhound can gather from numerous localities whole sackfuls of semi-precious stones, well worth the trouble of packing out, sorting up and polishing. He will find, too, a ready market for his better-grade specimens.

Gemstones such as agate, opals, and garnet; jasper, zircon, tourmaline; topazes and amethyst, are all there awaiting the diligent seeker. And today a bright new industry is building up in the polishing, cutting and setting of such stones.

Equally interesting to the collector are New Zealand's petrified woods, rare corals, and beautiful sea shells; the rainbow-coloured sands at Rotorua and other thermal areas; pumice (volcanic froth) and obsidian (volcanic glass) both of which occur in quantity at a number of places, and were used for many purposes by the Maori. About 50,000 tons of New Zealand pumice are processed commercially each year to make sandsoap, scouring powders and insulating material. Mayor Island, twenty-two miles from Tauranga, has a cliff of obsidian half a mile long, and the sands at its foot are studded with angular lumps of this dark-green glassy rock.

Industrial Minerals

Coal reserves adequate for the country's needs have been found in New Zealand and are mined in both islands. Most of today's mines are state-owned, are equipped with modern coal-winning machinery, and provide good pay and working conditions for employees.

Both underground and opencast methods of mining are used, but in New Zealand there are none of the deep shafts so common in other countries. Instead, tunnels are driven horizontally, or at a slight incline, into the seams, some of which are more than 100 feet thick. Mostly they range from six to twenty feet, so miners can work while standing upright. The annual output of New Zealand coal is around three million tons.

Many handsome building stones are quarried in New Zealand — marbles, limestones, granites, serpentine, and a range of dark volcanic rocks. Most prolific are the limestones, with some deposits over 2,000 feet deep. In all, these minerals constitute immense national wealth, to which most New Zealanders rarely give a thought, their importance in the public mind being eclipsed by the more spectacular operations of the oil-drillers, or the exploiters of hydro-electricity.

Seven cement works and over eighty limeworks process the limestone, and much is used in agriculture. Finer varieties, such as Oamaru "whitestone", grace the facades of imposing buildings, while lithographic limestone, on which engraving can be done, figures in their interior decoration. Only when New Zealand stops using so much wood for housing and other construction — or when steel becomes too costly — will her wealth of natural building stones be fully realised.

Today crushed rock, gravel and sand, used mostly for road-making and building, have a higher commercial value — about $20,000,000 yearly — than any other solid mineral item. Clays for brick-making are plentiful, while the finer kinds support a thriving ceramics industry. Clay modelling and pottery as an art form have a large following in New Zealand, the quality of the local work being high by world standards. Both islands have deposits of pure silica sand, used for making glass.

Steel

Until the late 1960s efforts to establish a steel industry based on New Zealand ores had not succeeded. To be sure, there are deposits of limonite (iron oxide) in several localities; and at Onekaka, near Nelson, 37,560 tons of pig iron were produced from the local ore between 1922 and 1935.

More rewarding are the vast deposits of ironsand piled up along the western beaches of both islands, where well over 500 million tons of high-grade ore is known to exist. From the very earliest days this immense source of potential wealth attracted the interest of settlers, especially at New Plymouth, where the renowned Mr E. M. ("Ironsand") Smith and others made determined efforts to smelt the sands.

Furthermore they succeeded in these efforts as far back as 1848, when a Cornishman named Perry, using a cleft in a cliff to make a forced draught, produced a quantity of iron which was forged locally into a variety of small articles. Further samples of pig iron were produced and sent to England, where they were turned into steel "of surpassing excellence".

In the 1850s some of this steel was tested by London and Sheffield cutlery firms and converted into razors, saws, scissors, pen-knives, surgical instruments, swords, and so on, the iron proving eminently suitable for these purposes because of the closeness of its grain, and its adaptability to producing steel of high flexibility, polish, toughness, and keenness of edge.

But the ore was also intractable. Impurities such as titanium oxide clogged the furnaces and thwarted all efforts to produce pig iron economically. Metcalf Smith invented a method of briquetting the sands with the local clays; and while this held out high promise of success, lack of capital and other difficulties brought these earlier efforts to naught.

Nevertheless, trials and researches have continued; new methods have evolved for refining and smelting the ore; and Government capital has been forthcoming. A New Zealand Iron and Steel Company has recently been formed and has inaugurated a multi-million dollar plant at Glenbrook, thirty-six miles south of Auckland. And so today, as a result of high faith, perseverance, and determination, another great commercial dream has come true for New Zealand.

CHAPTER TWENTY

Electricity

W ITH ITS ABUNDANT RAINFALL, high mountains, and numerous lakes and rivers New Zealand is well provided with natural resources for generating hydro-electricity. The production and distribution of electricity is, in fact, the country's largest industry. The State controls electrical generation, in which it had invested well over $600,000,000 by 1966. Local distributing authorities had invested a further $200,000,000; and additional large Government expenditure is envisaged to cope with a rapidly growing demand.

In both main islands a unified system of power stations, transmission lines, and substations ensures that electricity is available to more than 99.5 per cent of the total population.

In the South Island plans for the development of a multi-million dollar aluminium-smelting industry have now been based on the cheap and abundant water power available there. With this in view, and to reinforce the national supply, New Zealand's largest hydro-electricity undertaking has been developed at Lake Manapouri in Southland, with an envisaged potential of 700,000 kilowatts.

Power Cable

The next largest — and perhaps the most interesting — of New Zealand's hydro-electricity schemes is also in the South Island, at Benmore, mid-Canterbury, on the Waitaki River. There power is generated for transmission from the South Island where the hydro-electric potential is greater, to the North which has the larger population, and hence the greater demand.

Also, since South Island rivers generally run highest in the spring and summer, and those in the North in autumn and winter, the two Islands complement each other hydrolically.

In 1958 plans were drawn up for a submarine power cable

across Cook Strait, a distance of twenty-five miles. This cable was to be capable of carrying 600,000 kilowatts of electricity at 250,000 volts, direct current, and by the end of 1961 construction was under way at a total cost of £2,750,000 sterling.

At the end of 1964 the first phase was completed in the world's greatest project in power transmission — one which outclasses similar systems in British Columbia, the St Lawrence River, the Baltic Sea and the English Channel. The Channel link, for example, carries only 160,000 kilowatts at 200,000 volts, d.c.

Of the three power cables now crossing Cook Strait (there is also a telegraph-cable link) about 1,000 yards apart, one is a spare. All are gas-filled at a higher pressure than that of the greatest water-pressure (400 pounds per square inch) at the greatest depth (900 feet); so, if one is damaged no water can enter, and the cable will continue to function so long as nitrogen gas is available from the large reservoirs maintained at each end of the cable.

Vital to the whole system is a 2,700 feet dam across the Waitaki River, which has created a lake of thirty square miles. The energy created there by a 305 feet head of water is converted to direct current, which is transmitted overland by aerial cables. About 380 miles away, at Haywards substation north of Wellington city, the power is re-converted to alternating current. Converter equipment for this project cost six and a half million pounds sterling.

CHAPTER TWENTY-ONE

Gulf, Bridge And Harbour

S HIPS APPROACH THE CITY of Auckland via the magnificent Hauraki Gulf, 1,850 square miles of the South Pacific Ocean locked between two great arms of land which point approximately to the north. The Gulf is studded with scores of islands, some inhabited, and ranging in size from that of an English county to mere chunks of bare rock, perching-places for shags and other seabirds.

Several are volcanoes; and one — Rangitoto — guards the entrance to Waitemata Harbour. This harbour comprises a drowned valley system, oriented roughly east and west and debouching into the Hauraki Gulf. Along the southern shores of the Waitemata (usually translated as "Sparkling Waters") lie the port of Auckland and its adjacent commercial area.

When their ship ties up, passengers disembarking at Auckland cross gangways leading directly to a modern terminal building where entry procedures — Customs, and the like — are speedily put through, though some (e.g. the quarantine regulations) may take a little time.

These, in a country which depends heavily on its livestock, and which has a high regard for human health, receive rather more than perfunctory attention. They are, in fact, quite strictly policed; and all manner of articles which could be contaminated, even in the most innocent circumstances, are required to undergo fumigation, at a plant on a nearby wharf.

At Auckland the new arrival by sea is just a stone's throw from the Chief Post Office, at the foot of bustling Queen Street, one of the city's main business thoroughfares. Further up the harbour he may see the imposing Auckland Harbour Bridge — sometimes facetiously called the "Coathanger". Opened for traffic on 30 May 1959 this single-span reinforced concrete structure, with an overall length of 3,348 feet, links Point Erin on Auckland's south shore, to Stokes Point on the north shore, which has thriving urban clusters — the city of Takapuna, the boroughs of Northcote, Milford, Birkenhead, and Devonport.

Auckland's Harbour Bridge rests on piers sunk to depths of up to 104 feet, the main ones being built on caissons with their foundations in the Waitemata sandstone. An 800 feet navigation span rises 142 feet above high-water level. Mooted and discussed for about half a century before it was built, this bridge has now largely supplanted the ferry services which formerly took passengers and vehicles across, and it eliminates the need for driving thirty miles over a winding road connecting the two sides of the harbour.

Right from very earliest times the sparkling waters of the Waitemata, with their glorious setting of beach, cliff, sky, and alluring islands, have caught the imagination of men — coaxed them to venture out in boats, to fish, to trade, to race, to make war, or just to sail idly on the water.

First there were the Maoris, in their little one-man dugouts — or their mighty two-hulled structures holding 100 or more warriors. Then came the white men, with their whaleboats, cutters and scows, their brigs and schooners. They traded, raced and caroused, in an idyllic setting — one of the world's finest maritime playgrounds. And today every second Aucklander, from the schoolboy with his P-Class sailer to the businessman with his luxury yacht, his speedboat or his cabin cruiser, disports on the sunny Waitemata or ventures out on the broader Gulf.

Some ply even further afield, to Sydney, Hobart, Suva, and Samoa. Others seek the deep-sea fishing grounds round Mercury Island, Whangaroa, Houhora, and the Bay of Islands. And every year now, on Auckland's Anniversary Day, the world's biggest single-day regatta is staged on the Waitemata, where more than 1000 yachts and launches of every size assemble to compete in the many racing contests.

Competitors come from all parts of New Zealand, some from other countries. The day is a public holiday, in high summer, so thousands of people gather along the shores, pack the marine drives with vehicles, throng the cliff-tops, or sit at home with spyglass or binoculars to watch the races.

On other occasions Auckland citizens go down to the sea in ships, skim over it by hydrofoil, or fly in amphibious aircraft, on a multitude of missions . . . picnics on Motuihe or Waiheke Islands, weekends at Pakatoa, a modern holiday resort. or Waiheke, largest and most heavily populated of all the islands within the Hauraki Gulf, with its western end only ten miles from Auckland City. The name (meaning "Cascading Waters") is a dialect form of Waikiki, and this island has features strongly reminiscent of its Hawaiian namesake, in the form of numerous bays and beaches with sand, sea and sun (rain, too often enough) and long rollers curling in from the broad Pacific.

Its residents number some 2,000, of whom about 100 work in Auckland City, commuting daily by ferry. Some go by hydrofoil, but this costs more; and in emergencies, such as sickness or childbirth, (for the island has no hospital, though it does have a Government betting agency) residents can use an amphibious air service which gets them to the city in about ten minutes.

On Waiheke and some of the other islands farming is the chief occupation, though this is hampered, for most of them, by lack of suitable shipping services to clear their produce. Further out, some fifty-six miles north-eastwards from Auckland, lies the Great Barrier, largest of all the offshore islands and not actually within the Gulf but forming an extension of its eastern arm. Here fishing and crayfishing have been developed, while whaling, based on Whangaparapara Harbour, was recently but unsuccessfully tried out on a modern scale.

The early history of Great Barrier Island is a fascinating one, and bound up with it is the equally fascinating story of some of the Barrier's present families, for example the Medlands and the Blackwells, whose forebears settled there over 100 years ago on blocks of bushland of some forty or fifty acres. Lumbering was one of the earliest industries, and on Great Barrier the remains can still be seen of timbered dams, used to wash the mighty kauri logs down steep hillsides to the sea. Boats and ships were also built there.

Mining for copper and gold soon developed on Great Barrier, and with it a novel airmail service, claimed to be the world's first. Pigeons were trained to fly the sixty miles from this island to Auckland City, with messages written on tissue paper tied to their legs. This service began on 14 May 1897, long before the Wright brothers flew at Kittyhawk and continued for eleven years.

Each bird was stamped on the underwing with a number, the name of the service, and the address, so that a finder could return any bird which was lost or blown off its course. Each pigeon carried five messages, costing at first two shillings each. Such letters were carried in one direction only, so each week a steamer took a fresh supply of birds over to the island. The record time for the sixty-mile flight was fifty minutes, or seventy-two miles per hour. On 19 November 1898, special three-cornered stamps were issued for this Pigeongram Service — the forerunners of all modern airmail issues.

Other Gulf islands have their own especial interest, for example Little Barrier, now government-owned and strictly reserved as a bird sanctuary. Many native species, diminishing elsewhere, are able to multiply there; and they can be studied by bona fide naturalists with permission from the Department of Internal Affairs. Kawau Island, a scenic gem of four or five thousand acres, was once owned by Sir George Grey, who served two terms as Governor of New Zealand, and one as Prime Minister. His elegant home on Kawau has now been converted into a licensed tourist hotel, also owned by the New Zealand government, and is a favourite rendezvous for yachtsmen and tourists.

Grey paid £3,500 for his island paradise, which he stocked with wallabies, monkeys, ostriches, peacocks, and zebras. Today only the wallabies survive, along twih the ubiquitous opossum. Kookaburras, introduced from Australia, are also sometimes seen and heard there. Recently some dama wallabies, a species which had become rare or extinct in Australia, were sent to that country from Kawau Island, where the species continues to flourish.

Even less costly than Kawau was the little volcano close to Auckland known as Browns Island, which was bought in 1840 by John Logan Campbell (afterwards Sir John) and his partner William Brown. They gave in exchange for it twelve shirts, four double-barrelled guns, four casks of gunpowder, and fifty pounds in cash. Later this island was purchased by Sir Ernest Davis (now deceased) and presented to the people of Auckland, for use as a park. Browns Island has an exceptionally wide crater; and one wag has described it as "the only island in the world with a hole in it, and yet doesn't sink"!

INDEX

Oyster, 70, 107-8, 145

Pa, 20, 42, 48, 100
Pacific Ocean, 21, 30-2, 38-9, 44, 47, 63, 69, 130, 137-8, 151
Pakatoa Island, 153
Pakeha, 16, 35, 46, 54, 58, 93, 106, 109, 111
Pakeha-Maoris, 120
Palm (Nikau), 92
Pancake Rocks, 134
Papakura Gyseer, 84
Papakura, Maggie, 44
Parasitic Cone, 27
Parengarenga, 61
Paritutu, 119
Parliament, 37, 89
Parrot, 55, 57, 70
Parson Bird, 60
Paryphanta busbyi, 69
Passionfruit, 113, 115
Patu, 40
Paua, 106-7, 142-3
Pavlova (cake), 113-5
Pelorus Jack, 136
Pelorus Sound, 68, 135
Penwarden, Jim, 76
Perry (Ironmaster), 147
Pests, 78
Petrels, 67-8, 108
Petrified Forest, 134
Petroleum, 121-4
Petroleum, gas, 121, 123-4
Phormium tenax (N.Z. "flax"), 41, 43, 93-4
Pickering, Professor William, 17
Picton, 135
Piest'any, 83
Pigeons, 41
Pigeon Post, 153-4
Pigs, 39, 80, 99
Pig-hunting, 80
Pihanga (Mount), 127
Pineal Eye, 66
Pine-trees, 101-2
Pink and White Terraces, 28, 85
Pipi, 107
Planes, Amphibious, 75
Plenty, Bay of, 75
Pohutu Geyser, 84
Pohutukawa, 60, 95-6
Poi, 44
Poles, 32
Polynesian Culture, Settlement and Origins, 31, 37-9, 43-4, 47, 111, 139
Polynesian Society, Journal of the, 48-9
Population, 16
Porangahau, 125

Porina moth, 96-7
Porpoise, 70
Pouakai Range, 24
Precious Stones, 145
Priest Baths, 83
Prince of Wales Feathers (Geyser), 84
Pukaea, 45
Pukeiti, 24
Pukeko, 55
Pumoana, 45
Punakaiki, 134
Pupu Springs, 134
Pupurangi, 69
Puriri, 60
Putara, 45
Pygmy Pine, 95

Quarantine, 151
Queen Charlotte Sound, 135
Queenstown, 79, 132-3
Quinnat Salmon, 74

Rabbits, 78, 80-1, 99
Race Horses, 17-18
Racial Minorities, 31-2
Rainbow Trout, 72-3
Rainfall, 15
Rangitoto, 19-21, 151
Ranunculus, 25
Raoulia, 96
Rarotonga, 139
Rat, 39, 56, 61
Rata, 60, 95, 96
Raurimu Spiral, 124-5
Red Mountain, 134
Refrigeration, 99
Regatta, Auckland Anniversary Day, 152
Remarkable Range, 133
Resolution Island, 54
Richards, J. R., 118
Richardson, Professor L. R., 69-70
Rifleman, 64-5
Rimu, 102
Rites (Maori), 43
Rongomai, 47
Roosevelt, President Theodore, 78
Ross Dependency, 137
Rotomahana, 28
Rotorua, 18, 21, 28, 43, 72, 82-4, 102, 126, 146
Royal Marines, 36
Royal Navy, 88
Ruakuri Cave, 116, 118
Ruapehu, 21-3, 26, 82
Rugby Football, 17
Rutherford, Lord, 17
Rhynchocephalia, 66